Black Diamond in the Raw

MARVIN THOMAS

Ordering Information:
For orders and inquiries, please contact:
books@authorsnote360.com
www.authorsnote360.com

Printed in the United States of America

Acknowledgements

I would like to first give honors to the most high God for making this project a success and being patient through the years with me. Marketing Solutions and Events has made it possible to help so many businesses, business leaders and entrepreneurs. I'm grateful for this opportunity and trust that those that are in our network will rise to the occasion and take their rightful spot in the marketplace. To my beautiful wife Stacy, she has been my lifeline throughout the years and I owe everything I am to her and she has pushed me to do amazing things that I never would have envisioned for myself. I love her to the moon and back. My two stepdaughters Chellsea and Brittany King. I want to say thank you for being there for me and giving me hope. We laugh together and we cry together, that's what real family do. My mom Gloria Stokes has been a beacon of hope and my dad George Purvis a symbol of strength. Thank you both for your positive reinforcements. Thanks to my stepdad Jerry Stokes for being there for me from the time I was a kid up till now, much love and respect. A special thanks to Pastor Gregory Van Black, an inspiration to me and the embodiment of what a true friend suppose to be like, more like a true brother. To my sisters Tina Wright and Renee Stokes, I love you both dearly and thank you for keeping me focused on family even when I'm disconnected from everyone trying to build empires and kingdoms. Think, Think, Think, is what a brother from another mother told me, and I will remember your wise words forever, Claudius Grayson. To all my mentors that I think the world of Lynn Claiborne is the most renowned of them all, and Nikki Giovanni is my heart of poetry and thank you for being true guides in this dark world. My aunts and uncles that served as role models, I want to say thank you and I love you. My grandma Irene Brodie is our anchor and cornerstone in the Purvis family, and we love you so much. Special shout outs to my cousins Derrick, Det, Ty, Shawnee, Kevin, Dan, Cedric, Lois Ann, and Pam, Jermaine, and so many others that we were in the trenches together with. If I didn't get your name let me know to put it in the next book. Thanks to our great marketing team, all of our vendors, and IBO's that make our networking dreams come true. Everything is connected to everything. RIP to my grandma Ethel, she was the one that stayed praying for me. RIP to my grandfather Henry who taught me how to save money. RIP to my uncle James who showed me style, long live the Possum.

Facebook Pages: Msevents757, Msevents717, Msevents843, Msevents417, Msevents301, Msevents252
YouTube: Marketing Solutions and Events Thomas
Website: www.mseventsworldwide.com
Email. Msevents757@gmail.com

Contents

Chapter One

The Extreme Pressure of Perfection

In a world where everything is chaotic and confusing at every turn, the self-development business has never been so promising. In fact, I found myself in doubt in terms of making anything out of myself worth talking about, let alone writing about and advertising to the world. Life is a hardwork and we got to put the sweat equity in to be successful. The truth of the matter is the progress that I've made has taken a little more than hard work, it was extremely difficult to focus on the many things that I had to correct in my life to be someone that I could look at in old age and be proud of. Well if I'm lucky, because the afternoon I'm in right now isn't promise to me.

What if I told you that I was just like any other average Joe Blow that you see walking around every day without a lot of wisdom or forethought on any topic or had any mastery of any subject. Definite aim is the order of the day, no more small talk. One day in November of 2007 tons of earth and rock was dump and piled upon my knotty head and it was then as a larva wrapped softly in a cocoon that I began to transform my thought. Much like a Luna moth, being developed inside of this cocoon, which was for me; prison, I was released for a short time with a great purpose. I knew nothing of what all my journey would intel, but I prepared anyway. It was told to me a long time ago and somehow, I remember this quote, that it is better to be prepared for an opportunity and not have one than have an opportunity and not be prepared. In my cocoon I begin to do the unthinkable, while other inmates are trying to figure out how to get out of prison, I wanted further in. Obviously, large groups of people felt like I deserved to be in that rat—infested purgatory. Never-the-less, I was trying to figure out how to get out of time what would be to my advantage when I exited this cocoon. A 4year 10month hiatus isn't a lot of time to redirect a lifetime of destructive thinking but it was going to have to do.

My plan started in a very raw nature, as most people who know me, know I'm an ole country boy from North Carolina. I had no vision of what success looked like accept in the owner of Nathan Bryant's tobacco field and in evisceration lines of my local chicken factory Perdue Farms. I went on to have a lot of experiences that gave me the wisdom of a grumpy old man at a very young age. Inside me is a very old man who I will think of as Jack. Life hard lessons early on, I called the extreme pressure that pushed some of my thinking to perfection. The incarceration was just the icing on the coal caked up. In this Jewel book you will find a list of Jewels that do not have a simple value of knowledge from other people, but some that has come from my very own and makes it that much more valuable and sentimental. My joy is always the most precious and the simplest of joys which is to read and watch through as many men and women eyes as I can imagine, in way of positively changing lives forever. Even the most trivial and smallest Jewel may have the largest impact, remember that as you read through. The great motivational speaker that I love to listen to during my time here is Darren Hardy, who has created a term called the Compound effect. In my experiences all my decision has been compiled to end up eventually coming to the crossroads of one big decision.

Dedicated 2 Tracy Norman

Rest in Peace
Lil Angel

An angel we been in her presence
Just a few caught the sweet scent of her essence
The Joy that she brought was a blessing
To meet one that was sent straight from heaven
A spirit pure, she knew laughter was a cure
With her charms and allure, she was an angel for sure
Can someone explain this pain we must endure?
I'm thankful I knew her as a friend
Her wings underneath fluttered with wind
Then she rose up and flew in thin air
This?? Angel with enormous heart eager to share
Sincerely, your friend Marvin

Jewel 1. Today man steals a piece of candy, tomorrow he will attempt to steal the world. This is a very important lesson to start off with because it is necessary to understand that the little sweet innocent mistake of taking something that doesn't belongs to you can now surmount down the road of trying to pull off the unthinkable with many lives being affected.

One of my greatest accomplishments in life was finding my (why). This can be summed up as what is going to come next for me and how can I be the most prepared for it when it comes. Now to know the why, the what, where, when, and how's can come into play.

Jewel 2. For a person to live successful in today, he must constantly think 2 or 3 days ahead; at the very least. The most important lesson that I've ever gained from prison is being prepared, even if things didn't work out the way I expected to. Having the proper tools for the job you'll need a few days from now. When you have the tools or knowledge for a specific situation, then the law of attraction comes running from the back and says look let me make use of your tools with this opportunity. That is why when the day comes upon us and we are a couple of days ahead of it, then the additional information that we can apply to that day will propel us so much further in that day leading up toward success.

Jewel 3. The Elites rule the world. Elitist in life are habitual in the pursuit of knowledge. As it is habit to shower brush your teeth, and breathe, so is it the same with obtaining knowledge. It must be second nature and done without effort or much thought. Elites are a select part of a group that is superior to the rest in terms of ability or qualities. This mindset in my belief comes from those who have developed their craft and put 10,000 hrs. in a concentrated area. Like a gymnastic or a figurine ice skater who goes on to win the gold medal in the Olympics. The knowledge that needs to be acquired in bunches motivates them for what they know will come. Elites know what it will take to become excellent and this simply having all the information. Pushing forward beyond that to become phenomenal is the unlikely result but, without it in sight they know it will never happen. In the political and sociological theory, the elite (French elite, from Latin eligere) are a small group of powerful people who hold a disproportionate amount of wealth, privilege, political power, or skill in a society. Compacted in extreme pressure and intense heat through the duration of a said period will one gather the information needed to be conquered. Achieving high level of success has its dedication and commitment challenges. It requires a lot of ambition, effort, and drive that constantly pushes the person towards her hopes or dreams. There is something else that I've discovered that presses upon average people that allows them to do the things that we can only sit back and read or write about and that is being exposed to nothingness.

The most practical of decision comes with the least amount of thought that can remain true to oneself, however it is the critics and the pressure of friends and family that makes the decision so complicated in its politically correctness. Trying to satisfy the masses with an answer that may be selfish, but are questions that you can only honestly answer.

Jewel 4. If I was asked which I would rather allow to have sex with my wife, my enemy or my best friend; I would say which ever she chose, because at that point they both would be seen the same in my eyes. This may be a hard saying for any man to hear or be face with. The truth of the matter is that it happens every day unknowingly to the significant other. So, it's not as if there is a lesser monster to deal with just because you know and seen if you get to decide. It is a very basic decision to accept and move forward from if this thing had to be. Give the decision away or allow the impact of the damage to be as great on both ends. This my friend eliminates the tantalizing decision of worst-case scenario to even worst, which now won't matter. The affects are still the same and the two individuals, the best friend and the enemy has now become one.

Jewel 5. The most dangerous thing in the world is when a man has very little or nothing to lose. Have you ever watched a gangster movie and some maniac gunman shooting at someone shoots all through the crowd hitting innocent bystanders' women and children, and even cops ducking? It reminds me of the 1992 film Juice were Bishop attempted to shoot Q in an elevator full of people, or the 2007 film American Gangster were Frank Lucas shot someone dead in the street in front of everyone because he owed him a small amount of money. This mindset has become centered around lost, hurt, suffering and pain. When they are no longer threaten by these egregious events then what else is there. The person is locked in and forced to only see the conflicting object in mind and to go through with it despite the pain, suffering or lost that he or she may be all too familiar with. In fact, it may come down to the individual not even seeing it as hurt and pain anymore. It may start to feel good and doesn't hurt anymore to get the things needed done for so called pain. When all is lost and the only thing that is available is an objective in sight, the situation can come out to a lot of casualties on the other end.

Marcus Garvey said, Personal experience is not enough for a human to get all the useful knowledge of life, because the individual's life is too short. So, we must feed on the experience of others. Therefore, please understand through my experiences that I lived at a particular time with nothing to lose and during my federal case, my bond was denied because they said that I was dangerous.

Jewel 6. Good Judgment comes from experience a lot of that comes from bad Judgement, with life harsh realities and its cruel teaching through experience. First comes the test then comes the lesson. This one fact that I discovered during my life was that I could never get all the information that I desired to create the life I felt I deserved. Nor did I have the time or luxury to embark on the many different journeys to collect the most intrinsic parts to build the greatness that's known in the lives of others when solely committed to one task. The key is to allow others experiences to become your own, you learn from them, grow from them and share their story with empathy as if it was yours. We have access to hundreds of generations of stories that can impact each one of our lives if we embrace it as our own. The only problem is that we don't want to carry the weight of the pain that they carried. We only want to embellish ourselves in the success they may have brought to light without simply learning from their mistakes. It is a curious thing that we don't pick the brains of our parents more and make sure that the immediate dangers that may lay in front of us are made aware of. My father

George Purvis often told me how drinking excessively caused him to get a DUI and lose his license for quite some time. I followed right in his footsteps with a DUI of my own, but now with that experience to guide me, I know that driving completely drunk will never happen again. It is much to be said on this Jewel because of the decisions we make in life makes up the bulk of our destination in life. Just to leave you with this thought as I close this Jewel, when we hear someone say that an old wise man once told me this or that, remember he was once a young fool, and something had to have happened to wise him up, your challenge is to find out what that something was.

Jewel 7. To obtain greatness one must show great acts of sacrifice. We have all heard the sayings we are what we eat, and we become who we associate ourselves with. Greatness is an added value to a good feature; a cut above standard. We don't look at greatness the same normal way we look at something that is good. For example, I've been adding value to my good qualities of life such as language. I believe in this day and time everyone should be bilingual. This is the new standard that I've placed in my viewing because even I know Spanish which I learned in prison. Cuando fue la ultima vez que es ta vista la bibliotheca. Had I not had the 4 years and 10 months to study the language I probably wouldn't have gotten it either, but I also immersed myself in the library. Spanish speakers and the culture became my new focal point and my new friends were Mexicans and I was an Amigo. The process took time as I became a student, asking questions and taking the time to study, read and write it. Yuhimmu kam anta bati taalama annaka lan tatawaqqaf, Learning Egyptian Arabic has become my newest language to learn and my master teacher Amir is delighted to teach me. This gives me the ability to be seen in my own eyes as something better than average. This is how man or woman is recognized from the different social classes and valued more significantly than someone who speaks only one. This sacrifice of time must come to be for self-actualization of greatness and then the world will see you the same and embrace what may be brilliance to them but to you just mere sacrifice.

Jewel 8. If you're not willing to make choices in life, then life will choose for you, ever choice has a reward and a consequence.

Procrastination is the thief of all opportunities and it is tomorrow that never comes. In decision making concerning the things we should do, we wait around for the perfect opportunity gathering information and collecting data to make a sound decision. This will allow our decision to have negative consequence by default. When we don't answer or say anything we answer and are crying out something. Our actions become through inaction and this is in my opinion the picture that says a thousand words. For an example, if a wife asks her husband has, he been drinking, and he says nothing to defend himself, then the rule of thumb is that most likely he has been drinking and will be judge accordingly. The courts of the states act in similar ways in guilt and battle back and forth between sincerity and truth.

One of my favorite books I've read so far is the 33 strategies of War, by Robert Greene. War is a part of life along with peace and prosperity. It is up to the person to figure out if he will fight bravely for the victory of his warfare or go along with the program designed for mediocrity and slow self-development. This strategy keeps the masses of people slaves to a system called poverty. It enables the rich and wealthy elites to feed off the backs of these individuals with no hopes and dreams to dedicate their lives to accomplishing theirs. I've heard a motivational speaker by the name of Brian Tracy states if you do not set out to accomplish your own hopes and dreams then because you have none you are cursed to work for those who do.

Jewel 9. If I was to send someone to accomplish a mission that I was responsible for, after the person I've sent has left my sight. Then I would send someone after him to find out what is taking so long; and begin to think of his replacement. Contingency should always be the order of the day and without a solid, full proof back up plan for the backup plan then it shows that you don't take getting the objective accomplish serious. It is not that you don't trust the individual sent out to complete the task, it's just a slight way of reminding the person how important it is and before they can get settled in to what their priorities and objectives are, before they can fully embrace the task, this needed pressure added to what's taking so long makes it clear that humanly possible is the time frame of completion. My wife Stacy use to ask me after she sent me to the store, and I routinely took a bit longer than everyone else store visits because I'm usually chatting with the store clerks or taking the scenic route. It seems like times when she wanted to rush me, and I already knew to go straight there and back, before I get a mile down the road, she would call me and complain what's taking me so long. Luckily no replacement people ever flew past me while I was in route.

The extreme pressure of perfection has everything to do with diligence, TD Jakes said that diligence is what causes rocks to erode. The pecking of a drop of water on a stone will leave an impression if it is diligent. Every jewel and gem in collection shows the cuts, colors, and rarity of its kind making it the more precious.

Jewel 10. Prison is the greatest experience anyone can have next to death that hasn't come yet. If you can make it through such an experience and resume life back to normal or able to achieve greater then there truly is nothing beyond you that can't be done. This is the jewel many can't relate to because it lies at the opposite end of the spectrum of light. Prison to say is great doesn't mean in this sense that it was good, but powerful and overwhelming. Awesome in the sense meaning extremely impressive or daunting, meaning more daunting concerning this experience. Death can't be overcome, much like prison it is almost impossible but has a narrow window of escape. It is said with in the first 3 years is when most individuals released face recidivism and commit a crime landing them back into jail. 7/10 face this statistic and struggle to assimilate back into society and accepted back into their communities. Lastly the main point to remember about this jewel is the time frame that success must happen and being able to add the value to what it is that you are trying to add value to as quick as you can. We must find a way to put ourselves in position to win every day, to achieve our goals no matter how small or seemingly insignificant. This is the only way to see the big picture and accomplish the large dream. This brings me to the next jewel that has me self-conscious of time and each moment. Just the other night I was a little worried of not waking up in the morning because of a fluttering heart and a guilty conscious of not doing all I can do to make my life a better life with the time that I already have. What a scary thought to have everyone wake up to a dead body that is you and what's worse is that you had so much planned that you were going to do when you had the time. The moral of the story is do it now, do it now, if you have something that you are planning to do, then do it when the notion comes to mind like me writing this book at this very moment. Never know right, my days could be number and not make it to the end of the year which is only four months left at this present time. Trying to cross over to the end of the month could be as far as here right now to the moon.

Jewel 11. Can anyone recall the hours in the day they've lost or wasted back again; to add value and to make them productive. Life is a one-shot deal; even though, to consistently accomplish goals each day is a difficult endeavor, it is not impossible. Life has a strange way of pushing us pass the goal post when we have a dream in mind, and we pursue with extreme effort. The idea of pursuing dream and getting them in our view giving extreme effort which I look at as applying pressure to an open wound and then the results will come running like ER technicians and nurses. Production in the completion of the day are steady, consistent and with much effort and energy. This is how goals are accomplished.

Jewel 12. Even though some things seem funny, we must learn when to laugh. There's nothing amusing, the most laugh-able matters are so trivial and so quickly can turn deadly. This is the jewel that most people seem to think is a joke within itself. In prison a person can slap a person and even drag him across the floor in the fury of his anger and have everyone laugh till their bellies are sore and hurt. But it's only a matter of time, not even but a few days later that the gentleman that got dragged in the floor and slapped comes with some sharp object and almost mutilate the individual that did the act on him. With great sadness the family of the victim remember him as a good kid that always would fool around a little too much. His joking and playing caused him incarceration and then a burial service that no one in the family was ready for nor could afford.

Jewel 13. After coming to prison there's no going back to seeing life as it once was, if you've experienced self-discovery. Being on this side will develop, an intense hunger, those on the

other side will call this ambition, Con artist will use it to further manipulate, the business savvy will use it to further excel. I never had an idea that having my freedom taking away from me would create a sense of urgency in me that would make me want to view my life at the end. It is impossible to live completely in the moment all the time. In fact, it is my opinion that we must come to terms with who we are as individuals and then move in life accordingly. It was when I was in my early 20's when I smoked too much marijuana and became very paranoid. I chase a piece of paper around the yard for about 3 to 5 minutes when then I realized that I was being watched and laughed at by two old men in their 80's. I begin to laugh too, but the entire scene became grossly embarrassing and I couldn't do any-thing else but to get away from them two rascals. I for a split second seen myself as an old man trying to capture the wind and it eluded me, and I knew that the nature of life was upon me at that moment and it would come to visit me again, but the next time it would be real and it would be no going back to the activity that I have with my limbs now, or my mental capacity to think. The older gentleman that laughed at me was Jack Howard, my father in law at the time and he is worthy to be mentioned because he looked me into my eyes and with a nod from his steely old eyes gave me the confirmation that he had seen me and that I needed to get to work quickly at whatever it was that I was trying to do with my life.

Jewel 14. To have experienced love for one second can be enough to last a lifetime. It is to my best understanding that most people want to be happy over the experiences of their lifetime, it is the consensus after interviewing multiple people that to have the realness of a relationship is far better than to be in a fake on. It is therefore just as important to know while in a real relationship that they may be willing to trade one day for, in exchange for a relation-ship maybe with a beauty queen that isn't for-filling is not worth the time of any person. True love is pure and unforgettable and to feel that just once, can quickly be exchange for an arm charm and a woman that possible gives you status and statue.

What a Scene Eyez Seen

Eyez seen you through Iron Strings of a barb wire dream catcher.
Through my eyez at the beach looking atcha
Mesmerized by your hazel nut eyez
I sent you a sweet-scented read rose through rock solid concrete.
Ready to descend deep as a starfish laying
on the bed of the ocean of your soul.
Dreams of my trust inside you, I want
it as bad as I want to breathe
As a Luna Moth I want this moment forever,
Because we are briefly together B4 we
are weak, then we must leave.
So as Eagles I imagined our talons locked in the air
Swirling around as we come down in
fleeting winds without a care.
Bear in mind we were both pushed in and
released like dolphins in the waves.
I gazed out and seen you in this scene through
iron strings of a barb wire dream catcher.

Jewel 15. Once a man becomes possessed with an idea, it is almost impossible for him to return to a reality without that idea. This is a similar method that some people get confused with infatuation, or obsession. Like the books that we write like I'm writing now, or when we decide we are going back to school for a degree. It comes with a compelling force that drives the individual to complete her task with little effort. Almost every goal is achieved by being goal oriented. Like a baby learning how to take steps for the first time. These steps are kind of ordered by the parents as they are coerced and lead by them. This feeling of being lifted gives the baby future runner a shot of dopamine and I think Mikey likes it. She produces enough courage to continue to walk future on her own till her strengths gives out of her legs and then she falls. This process could happen thousands of times, but the idea of walking never leaves the little growing baby reality and can never go back to crawling real fast all over the place as if she has arrived at greatness. Then one day as it was the dopamine that gave her the feel-good shots to try again, she begins to cover the entire length of the living room and then make it to the kitchen and so on and so forth. The reality only grows bigger from their and her world. So, is it with a man and his baby idea? It must grow and become strong and begin to do for itself. To not acknowledge such a thing would be equivalent to a man having a clear vision of how to make a million dollars and then roll back over and go to sleep and never think about it again.

Jewel 16. The two most powerful weapons to be used in the art of war are to be armed with friendship and alliances, also to know your enemy strengths and weakness. In war it is almost synonymous with drugs, poverty, crime and elite manners on finance. This is what war is all about, taking over land that may have resources that the stronger opposition can use for their good, or the people to work as slaves or use of ideas that will put the other side in a better position. It is prevalent that in war you use both tactics as much as you can. It is seen in movies where sometimes the alliances move back and forth in between enemy lines to prove loyalty to one side or the other, and in playing in some cases both sides then it becomes a massacre and both sides lose, and the friend having been friends with one side and maybe family with the other destroys both sides. This same method is also used in seduction when trying to seduce a man or a woman. It is the cunning art to overtake, conquer, and win the heart of the victim that has been chosen. This sometimes means war and will amount to using the things in her life that has not allowed you to fulfill your mission as the enemy, and you may find yourself trying to find all the help you can get. He or she may not be won over easily, and some people have even used the help of God to fight their battles, so they can obtain what they want. In War clever tricks are used to expose the opponent, such as betrayal, love and ruthless strategies to win and accomplish the mission.

Jewel 17. Let us use brevity in the delivery of speech, instead of beating around the bush with lofty words that are many, to do the work of few. We are living in a time now that everyone wants to be smarter than what they really are, so that is why schools are profiting so largely. Workshops and seminar are on the rise in terms of making people feel a bit more self-discovered that want to be a millionaire. So, it has been what I've seen and translated that people have been stuck delivering lengthy monologues and reciting dissertations to explain something as short and sweet as to say people take all day to say what they got to say. Big words do showcase a variety of vocabulary and tells in some detail about a person, in his professional field, whether it's politics, business, medical or even religion. These expressions and mannerisms added explains the person and, in some cases, forces you to focus on them in which they may not have had any attention paid on them in a while. It is more than unnecessary to over explain in dialogue with a bunch of words when brief words can be used to hurry and answer question. The eloquent speaking of a person doesn't guarantee the accuracy of content.

Jewel 18. Rarely, a genius will be recognized during his life-time. Often, they'll go unknown until decades down the road. Only then will his or her work begin to seem profound. This is the most common thing that our civilization has been challenged with and will always face in recognizing genius. It is seen in sports, artistry, politics, business, and religion. There is genius maybe in you, but even after all your accomplishments that you are making today it will never be talked about and dissected as it would be until you have passed form. Steve Jobs the businessman was not only great in his innovation of the iPhone and other apple products that we still use today. His genius is expressed through his clarity of developing the singular objective and focusing on not the many but the few. He poured his passion into this one objective and masterfully his legacy still breathes among us with excellence. Even Tupac who himself influenced me in the artistry of poetry wasn't because at the times he was so great, but that he leads me back through a path of greatness. Speaking greats such as Maya Angelo, and even further to Vincent Van Gough. Our ability to understand the pass holds the significant keys to opening our future. I truly in my heart believe that this is the core of the extreme pressure to perfection. It's not that one man will arrive but will spark the mind of another and then down the generation down to another, and in the event of one's departure, leave a few more bread crumbs to complete the task given to him by this inner program that can't be explained to express the genius of humanity. Even in religion, the many different forms thereof have now begun to find its way back to the source, and whether it's ALLAH, God, Jehovah, or Buddha the aspiration of peace is upon us and violence and turmoil is not at our core values like in medieval times. Geniuses like Langston Hughes, Malcom X, Barrack Obama, Steve Jobs, Napoleon Bonaparte and so many more were never discovered their greatness until their death. The extreme pressure that produces excellence is what individuals gifted with the where with all to perform in the end the necessary ability to do what others can only dream about their entire lives. That my dear is bringing a craft into perfection.

Jewel 19. If you think you may not have an enemy, assume it's possible you have one you don't know of, or have forgotten about. But if you have wronged someone for sure, without making reconciliation. Then until you do reconcile walk with caution and assume, he is an enemy rather than a friend; also consider it possible that such a one may have at least twenty friends ready to turn on you. Apart from just having a plain enemy that wants to rip your head off no soon they see you and you want to do the same to them, the sneaky friend that has a grudge is even more dangerous.

Betrayal is the most cunning way to destroy a person, especially when the trusting heart must look in the eyes of, he who betrayed him and even sometimes parish with the thoughts of why. There was a friend of mine at the time who now will remain nameless but was more than a best friend he was like my brother. To use the language of brevity and allow few words to do the work of many, so we became at odds over a dispute over a crime we committed. My partner in crime virtually got away and I knew of his where about and possible hiding. Police after some others involved in our case gave up just enough details to lead them to asking me, I thought you said you didn't know this guy. I finally answered yes, in which they knew already where he was and were already in the process of picking him up but wanted my verification that he was indeed the gentleman that was our friend. I knew with everyone pointing the finger that it would lead to more trouble if I myself didn't come clean like everyone else. Despite all our testimonies, I was singled out and blamed by him on Facebook to have snatched away his freedom and his baby momma at the time. It was just seen by me as an outlet for him to vent on social media, but I took it to heart, and with precaution that in the event of his silliness, that a lot of people could have got hurt. It was very necessary to have this old friend as my enemy, and in a perfect world us two could sit down at a table and discuss how we intend to destroy one another if certain demands weren't met to reconcile the situation. Now we are as a people reduce to back biting and silent hatred. When a person knows this burden is constantly upon him then they will never again walk in ignorance and without caution of danger which is always lurking around the next corner where we sit perhaps idle waiting for something good to come.

Jewel 20. To think of my true friend makes me smile with pride to call them my friend. Their acquaintance gives me resolution, their advice redefines areas in my life in a way had it not been for my friend, these areas would have been left undiscovered. With a true friend in your life, it's sure to make you a better person. When I thought of this Jewel I immediately thought of my friend and sent them a text. This is what true friendship means in my opinion. It will make you think of them and make you laugh and smile. I think on the other hand that just because you feel a certain way about a person that you consider your friend that they might not feel the same way about you. It is almost like a courtship or a relationship of lovers. You meet the individual, then you find your commonality and then build off experiences whether through hardship or prosperity. In my opinion it takes a set of rules to get to the level that I acknowledge you as a friend and it is a joint custody of merits and favors done for one another. In this generation of friendship, most people only have the one-way friendship, where I do for you and I'll receive that endowment coming from my friend, but if they ask me for anything then I don't get anything for you. What a shame people don't use the power of friendship more often

Facebook has watered down the experience of friendship just a bit by never giving the participants education of what the extension of friendship is, not liking enough pictures to send a friend request to accept. It is not having to always talk through some chat line when face to face is available or at the very least an actual phone conversation. It is my best guess that a true friend you will do almost anything for, within your power. You live with their quirks and imperfections, and still love them unconditionally without a sense of worry or frustration. In closing I truly have a deep admiration for the few true friends that I have and can count on one hand, and that is why I chose to go into deeper detail of friendship because, of the severity of its non-usage and the lack of its authentication. How sweet and refreshing is it to be able to spend time with your friend.

Jewel 21. If I was forced to judge a man I had never known, first I would ask of his upbringing, then I would ask now to show me his friends. This Jewel is profound in so many ways due to past statistic and experiences that always prove in the law of probabilities, you are more compatible with who you spend your time with more than you think. The old saying goes two birds of a feather flock together. Our natural environments that we are raised in does shape our reality a present to us the future that we are willing to live with. There are factors to look at dealing with people characteristic, traits, and temperaments. When seeing the tendencies of a person and seeing the desires of their efforts, then judging becomes very easy. For an example, if you see an overweight person comes inside of a Barnes and Nobles bookstore, it can be judge upon him that he either loves coffee, reading books or need Wi Fi also that he loves to eat. To judge someone properly is to access the tangible and foreseen properties that exist in the individual. Sometimes misdiagnoses are inevitable because, a man on the street corner with dirty clothes and begging for money may use his sign that the world is coming to an end, God bless for the help. This individual could be using this platform as a misrepresentation of his actual selling of drugs and being a millionaire. The bible says judge not that ye might not be judge, but truth also is don't take it personal but if you are able to handle the judgement upon yourself then judge away.

Jewel 22. To forgive is to forget. Simple short and sweet but listen to me what I need you to understand is the simplicity of this quote doesn't take away from the complexity that it causes when forgiving doesn't produce the results of forgiveness. When you forgive truly there is a piece of yourself that will surrender the grief, pain, betrayal or whatever the disappointment was to settle the difference. Further decision would not be affected by the thoughts of the past. If I have wronged anyone that I know at any point, I'm letting you know through these writings that I forgive you and I forget those things which are behind me. I still may have to pay for some wrongs that I may have done in life, even if someone forgave me.

Jewel 23. Sanity is not a given characteristic or trait that everyone is born with. A sound mind comes with much responsibility, which must be enhanced, grown, and developed carefully over time. I think everyone in life in my opinion makes a conscious decision to be sane and rational. In the process of upbringing, choices are put before everyone that will allow that person to gather themselves through experience and what is at that time either socially accepted or how to survive in the environment of tolerance outside of the bounds of the norm. Now these so-called norms maybe as irrational as the insanity of doing the complete same thing more than once expecting different results, or cultural shocking to everyone else that is not a part of that cultural such as marriage of close relatives or even cannibalism. These are bounds of living that most people don't practice but in a few cultural this is perfectly fine. It is my best guess that in addition to this widespread mind shift people are exposed to and accept as normal, so is it when television world is pervasive in the home and individuals are able to distinguish characters in the movies from the real life and take whole of some of their personalities that are broadcast to them and act out in the way of sanity or of being insane. In closing it could be as simple as being kids and running with the toy guns playing cops and robbers. If a person is competitive and wants to win, then he knows at the end of his role he's going down. A large majority of the time the cops win out, leaving the robber to be placed in over packed prisons. It is my suggestion as kids that may stumble across this read to never want to play the robber or the bad guy period. It was a common expression to me growing up that good guys finish last, and that, it was a weird thing to go through life without having done several foolish acts that would conclude that I was a cool awesome guy. This was the biggest lie that had ever told me, or I could have ever believed. First, the good guy may finish last in the bad girls view but, where is she going to be when you're locked up. Maybe writing letters back and forth for a time but usually with the good guy, he has made the right decision to get a good job and maintain a stable life. It's possible that when you are released from jail or prison that she may leave the good guy and come back to what's familiar, but what a shortchange life to have to live with a significant other for the sake of not wanting to be a good boy. Next knowing that the law of average gives us a heads up that when we commit crimes that we are often to get caught, so why continue a life of crime. It has given gangster power to achieve great levels of success and some went straight, others could never find the right path. There also are plain evil and have found this lifestyle to be normal as having two hands and feet. The truth of the matter is what behavior will we accept from ourselves socially, and how are we going to adjust to the public and their standards of what it should be like. We develop these habits as we speak, tend to live with the results and hope at the end of the day they say Marvin Thomas was a good man, or honest man or even a fun-loving person, but to have them call you crazy mad man should never be our dreams of how we are remembered.

Long Live the Golden Rose

I fell in love with a golden rose leaf
Her divine vines were intertwined as a gold wreath
smothered golden petals unravel and unfold free
Resilient 24 karat gold stems console me
Then your beauty burst shine as a
shooting star leaving me blinded
Seething out your freshly cut pours is your love refined
At the tip of mountains never mined there's a bud deep within
And the little thorn erupts molten lava
and flows like fleeting winds
Till the entire rose is gilded causes harmonic
sounds like wind chimes
Rhythmic harping as a thousand frogs at dusk
around a pond in Malaysia climes
To max levels;
Pound softly in ears define this arrangement of priceless display
And wrapped warm in this hand as a blanket
lay a gold rose leaf inside a bouquet

Jewel 24. Death is the biggest mystery of all time. No one knows what really happens, only one can speculate through scientific theories and religion philosophies. Till that certain day comes when our heart beats no more, only then will we know for sure. It is some thoughts that when you're dead you're done, or that when it's over you end up in some type of oblivion. I'm more inclined to believe that we are beings of energy that cannot be created nor destroyed, so we eternally exist. I imagined the life of so-called death as with our eye's cloths and our voices there to keep us company. Like a sperm cell fighting to get past 9 million of his brothers and sisters to become the one. It is millions of years of evolution that happens in the womb as the egg is well prepared to produce the human body. Then genetics step in and give us eye color, skin complexion, body build and so on and so forth. Then we develop through our environments to become the person that we are today. It is through our final course of life that we become the person or being that we will be throughout eternity. Lastly to say about death the freaky subject that no one wants to speak about because we don't understand enough about it. I realize that by seeing how most Christians want to go to heaven but not one is ready to die before what they call their time. In fact, why die and be with God and you have all this earth to roam is what I think the feeling of the general population has. It is some secs Muslims that have quite a different view, where in death they will have seven virgins and live in a paradise.

Close your eyes in a silent place and death is upon you, we have different religions which we all have different belief. The mystery will never be known to us on this side and when we do final begin to unravel the mysteries of death then all the thesis and dissertation that we could possible write on it to explain the fears and the anxiety of it all will not be able to be sent back to the living. So, we agonize about the unknown for as long as we can and when we become too old to fully worry or care about it all then we become brave enough to look up and stare at the realness in front of us, we call this facing death.

Jewel 25. Many have only themselves fooled, and not even close to convincing their family and friends that they have changed. Unless you have calculated steps to achieve your goals

and dreams to show, no one will see your expectation nor take you seriously. Those who leave prison in such a way, without calculated steps and a divine change of heart, rush back to society to their own destruction. Most people call home and tell their family and friends that they have this dream of coming home and becoming a millionaire. It is a cute thing to here of such great news from someone that never had anything going for them now wants to be an entrepreneur. It is so important to not only have the willingness to tell people that you have decided to do something, it is prevalent that you put effort and action behind the word. No planning involved, nothing that will give any rational sane person the inclination that you are really going through with this idea of trying to become successful. When I was locked up the closest that I came to see some one that was trying to really come home and achieve their dreams was a guy name Rock that had a picture cut out of a lawn mower in his files. It was a funny sight to look at as if the actual lawn mower that he had cut out he was going to get. It was also humorous because he still had a few more years, and before he showed me potential areas that he could scout or banks that he could ask for a certain amount of money that would allow him to start up the business. It was in my first year that I decided that I wanted to write a book, and after that I spent the rest of my time preparing for the outcome of the finish product. I started writing rough drafts and editing schemes along with manuals after manuals of what I may use and what I would use. After all my work, I still needed money to get the work done, so I started saving money like crazy so that I could have a fighting chance. This was just the beginning because I still had so much to learn, and with all my research and editorial prowess it still took me a few minutes after release to figure it out. That journey was just an example of how one goal can lead you to accomplish so many things just to accomplish the one goal. Jim Rohan often said that becoming a millionaire is not just arriving with a million dollars but what it will make of you to become that millionaire is what is the most valuable of all.

Jewel 26. The only evil in the world is ignorance, a sworn enemy to wisdom. Any person claiming to be wise and over looks

this truth, is certain to be doomed. This one truth is the maxim of them all because this construction of this book is about absorbing the positive energy and truth of life and becoming a better person. Truth and knowledge skillfully used is the wisdom that many seek and often we don't have the time or luxury to achieve this knowledge all by ourselves and then to digest it and make it practical in our lives many will believe is just plain nonsense. To be ignorant is as evil as it comes, such as racism and discrimination for an example, with no accurate knowledge that makes sense about why to hate another person without a cause is foolish. Wisdom and ignorance cannot get along for any set period because they will ultimately cancel one another out. In fact, they war with one another constantly trying to impose their will on the other.

Jewel 27. The only reality worse than death is living in constant terror; in the event one should search for death and cannot find it, this goes beyond terror. A jewel such as this may not resonate until the time comes when it happens. It happens on the battlefield, in domestic violence reality, and even in some school or jail and prison systems. It can be identified by those who in the end commit suicide. Therefore, they come to terms with death because the terror that they reside in is far worst and easier to deal with.

Jewel 28. Nothing in life is ever simple. Even in the blink of an eye thoughts must hurry along and travel at 24 billion miles per second. Then through millions of nerves ending to the eye lid muscle to relax and contract if it is safe to do so. This is the growing phenomenal of our human experience, our bodies are so complex and without much thought carry out the most complex functions. It is amazing to have so many different things going on at one time. For an example I'm writing this chapter, listening to Simon Sinek and back and forth with my mentor Lynne Claiborne getting a speech ready for the next week. Not to mention other thoughts running through my mind that I am categorizing and prioritizing in the direction to do next, also really should be eating a sandwich. Multiplicity is the spice of life when you can decide what is the most import function you could be doing besides breathing.

Jewel 29. I'll rather hold on to a real ugly woman, than to envision I'll hold on to a beautiful dream girl. The facts of reality have a sick twisted sense of humor. It seems that most of the time we can enjoy the things that are in front of us that may have been a little difficult to obtain but it is what we are most comfortable with. It is also most what we believe we can have. I'm not a scrooge and telling you not to desire nice things and dream, the truth of the matter is that we must know our limitations and know the balance that we live in so that we are able to move accordingly. It is also my suggestion that we at any moment can move forward after we gain the where with all and become skilled in the knowledge, of self-development. The fact of the matter is the ugly woman is real, and the dream girl is just that a dream. Never stop dreaming and never compromise what it is that you want but challenge yourself too in the meanwhile hold on to something and figure out why the dream girl that is so beautiful has not succumb to the law of attraction or averages.

Jewel 30. We all shape our own fate; guide our own destiny; and lead ourselves to a heaven or hell that's buried deep within our hearts. As humans we often are triggered by the external and the tangible. So, we go to church and hang out for a few hours to hear about a place called heaven and hell and that we will inversely end up in one of these places. So, we spend the rest of our lives coming into the knowledge of this truth trying to avoid the one thing and in perpetual hesitation to arrive at the other. In the meantime, very, few people have pointed the finger at themselves. In fact, this is the only way to find out what your life will become. Because of our own actions, that leads us to the places we end up in life rather good or bad. Some of the actions could be a point that is neither good nor bad depending on if the individual is content with the way her life is going.

Jewel 31. It's hard to detect a bad person when you're constantly looking for the good in them. Some people are just awful people and hide behind a mask of good intentions. They know their true motive will be deflected if their faults are looked beyond and in them is searched out their best. The most moving aspect of a person is when they perform the good to others, and connection of positivity. The terrible news is the manipulation tactics that people use to compel people to do whatever it is that they want. When this is discovered then it is a shocking reveal when we only seen the good. It is like a child that has never been into any trouble and when the principle calls the parents and tell them of some negative act that the child has done, most of the time the parent goes into blame mood. Looking at who did what to her baby. This is true in fact because awful men started out most of them as awful little boys and continued to hide this fact by some sweet mask worn to cover their wicked deeds. So, most people as I was around thousands of them in prison during the beginning of the great recession of 2007 to 2012. These inmates often wanted the parole board to see them in a brighter light by doing good deeds, oppose to seeing the awful deed that landed them there.

Jewel 32. In life man chooses a role to play that he believes is befitting to his peers, then he rehearses the script until he becomes lost in his radiant character. Then he loses himself on the world stages. All humans in our society devote themselves to a cause and a script that is presented to them is read, like and rehearsed for the part. Some people watch television and see something that inspires them or hear something in song. Next after the role is accepted then the character is developed and communication with those that have roles in this grand play called life. Some have lead parts and others are extras that are not even utilized in the growth and development of who you are. The world sees us as whoever we have shown them and now the experience of being that must be sold to the world by masterfully and exquisite acting or action.

Jewel 33. A person who doesn't keep his word or tries is worse than a liar; for he builds hope and inspires commitment. Then with a single blow of inconsideration has betrayed trust with manipulation. This scoundrel doesn't mean what he says nor say what he means. To my understanding from my own personal experience, there is nothing more hurtful than being lied to or having the let down by someone you trusted to do something that you needed done. It is by no mistake that we gravitate to those few people in our lives that keep their word. It is almost like the sanctuary of life when you can depend on someone to come through for you. Even if you see a person trying their hardest to accomplish some goal for you and fail, it gives you a sense of relief that you have surrounded yourself around the right people. No one wants to be involved in a relationship where you can't depend on the person to do what they said they are going to do.

Chapter Two

Know Thyself

It is the journey of life to know who you are, it is a shame more people never question the why. Why is it so important that we learn everything about our unique selves? We are wonderfully constructed and have no sense of the amazing features that we can add to ourselves to perfect the temple of man. Socrates say, as he did in Phaedrus, that people make themselves appear ridiculous when they are trying to know obscure things before, they know themselves. Plato also allude to the fact that understanding thyself would have a greater yielded factor of understanding the nature of a human being. In the stones at the top entrance of the Temple of Apollo Delphi, it is engraved in Greek, Gnosis si upsom which simply means Man Know Thyself, and at the entrance ways of the Great Pyramids at the doorway it is written Tement noscis which means also know thyself. This to me means understanding one's self and having a larger overview of who you are. Yet have a deeper since of your being and the source of your power, your gifts, your true skills and abilities to do whatever it is that your destiny has purposed you to be. Let us consider the story of the Golden Buddha. In 1957, monks were commissioned the great task of moving this clay Buddha from one side of Thailand to the other. In the process of the move, there was noticed a crack in the massive work of art. They lifted it back down and decided to move it the next day. Later, that night a monk came out and shined his flashlight inside of the tent where they were keeping it and low and behold a light reflected at him. His curiosity would not allow him to believe that perhaps a fragment of some sort was wedged in the crack, so he got his chisel and hammer and begin to chip away. Before long what he had in front of him was a Golden Buddha. It was theorized that 300 years prior that the Burmese Army was attacking that part of Thailand and with no means of moving the large stature which stood 10 ½ feet tall, that the only way to keep it from being pillaged and becoming spoils of war, they covered it in clay and change the nature of the Buddha from gold to clay. The Burmese Army marched on to kill all the remaining monks, so the secret died with them. This is the lesson of self-discovery and that we must chisel away the clay and stone from around our hearts and minds. These are the influences of the world and the image that is placed upon us and not withdrawn from ourselves. While we look at our little growing babies and say she's going to be a great Dr. or Lawyer, or even scientist, the truth is that they should be given time and space to discover their own talent and abilities.

After I ate your Apple

Another flawless masterpiece worth millions
to hang in the mansion of my mind

You are forever enriching my soul with your
bold beauty busting complete radiance

Only the sun is slightly brighter when it shines

Perfection has no place beside you, it must
bow its knee in your presence

It's a peasant to your true nature, that's
why I wore cloths of the Gods

And I sipped from between your thighs
and stirred with a gold rod

So, in the future I will break springs until we both fall

Walls will be crunching and down to earth we will cum

Till there's nothing else left at all.

In Ancient Khemet, today known as Egypt, above the entrance of each temple and lodge serving as an academic and scientific learning center, appeared the phrase: Man Know thyself. Since we live in an age that is gender driven, we refer to the ancient saying as know thyself. The knowledge of self has always been the root of a complete and through education in the ancient Khemetic education of Initiation System (called the Mystery System by western historians). Lastly, I want it known that most of the prominent Greek philosophers and scholars got their training and information from studying in ancient Egyptians tombs and lodges. Philosophers that went by the name of Herodotus, the Greek father of History, in which he spent 23 years attending schools in ancient Egypt. These names also include the likes of Thales, Anaximander, Pythagoras and Solon. Lastly, the quote I want to leave with you on this very day, and I hope that you don't read quickly over it and pass on to the next rite of passage without fully allowing these read words to affect you in positive way. The quote goes as such, Socrates said that," The unexamined life is not worth living."

Jewel 34. The worst epidemic facing the African American community is not aids but procrastination. I have learned a long time ago that even when we wait, we need to hustle, in another words, find something to do while we are waiting on one goal to be accomplishing to work on what's next after the goal is accomplished. African Americans has got a bad rap for not living up to getting things done in a timely manner. In fact, during this generation and time black comedians joke about the different times associated with white people and black people often leaving people to believe that most black people are late and do not honor the same time everyone else honor. The sad truth is that African Americans begin to believe in this foolishness because no one was there to teach us to know thyself. If we are not taught who we really are then someone will come along and hand us a script and rather it be from television or listening on the radio, we will look over it and then decide on a role. Procrastination is not in our blood, but it is written in a script that we as African Americans have believed is the truth, and we have accepted it and jump out on the world stage with the excuse of this is just who I am. Aids can never affect as many lives without physical contact.

Jewel 35. No matter how much you have heard about a man, or seen for yourself, you still can never know him unless you have walked in his shoes. The truth about this Jewel is you never really know a person man or woman. The shared experience is what binds us and connects us to a human bond that gives us the understanding of who each other really is. Another truth sometime that goes unnoticed is a person shows us what they want to show us and even go on for decades being something that they are not. Then the moment of truth comes and reveals to us that we have only walked beside this individual and not where they have walked so when they jump off the bridge, it may be difficult for you to have the same faith.

Jewel 36. Morality is only as good as the condition of its environment. When these good conditions become breached then moral values become threaten. Then that good in the person could turn on him, or he could take his chances and fight in his cruel world with cruelty. Either way if he doesn't change his environment all hell will break loose. Simply put, everyone has a moral and value system that could be compromised at any time depending on the depth of the change of their environment. I'm reminded of the sweet innocent girl that grew up in the country, raised by her grandma and often went to church. As time moved on, she received a scholarship to a college that was in the city and was forced to leave home and go to an environment that she was not equipped or suited for by her family. A few low lives decide to manipulate her and prey on her innocence, by taking her to a party and slipping alcohol in her drinks till she is unconscious and date raped. It doesn't stop there because to many girls raped bounce back from date rape, so the new thing is pushing drugs into their system to make it harder for her to come clean. While she thinks it's her fault the low lives continue to pray on her with more drugs and more routine sex, that now have her in a trap to offer more sex to more guys to get the drugs. Now with this new environment introduce and the graduation of college becoming far-fetched, now it's committing crimes and God know what else. She couldn't fight back with goodness or she used the cruelty that was thrust upon her in indecent proportions. The moral of the story is unless she becomes free from this environment, like check herself into detox then it is most likely that eventually all hell will break loose for her.

Jewel 37. The old saying goes, you can lead a horse to the well, but you can't make him drink. This is because you've given him too many sips along the way. The man referred to as the horse must be given less than what he needs, and sometimes strung along by empty promises to keep him going; and if by chance he doesn't perish from dehydration, or whatever he lacks when he arrives to the well; OH, He'll Drink alright. This is a very powerful Jewel, because it's about a person that you can do all you can for and when the time comes for that individual to do what they are supposed to, even if it's for their own benefit it isn't common for them to drop the ball and not do at all what they can. This represent those that are in school, husbands and wives trying to hold the marriage together alone, business's that get advice from reliable sources just to try to branch out after they get on their feet only to fall again. It reminds me of a 9/5 job where they pay you during this era around $10-12.50 if you're lucky. This is promising for the worker in terms of getting raises and measly bonuses. But if you were to pay the individual more than they are worth then they perhaps may begin to miss days and perform not as great of task because the hunger is not there. Keep a man hungry and thirsty, the acts they will perform will be legendary.

Jewel 38. Brilliance sometimes must be downplayed to subtly accomplish what you will. Less one is made to raise up and show the world, your nay Sayers with opposition will never see it coming. In the 48 laws of power by Robert Greene, the 1st law is stated to never outshine the master. In retrospect this show of brilliance in ancient times could get you killed even if you meant well or even by show of brilliance saved lives. It is to my knowledge, that talent is used to the benefit of the wise without having to have to be worried about being undermined and undercut by their own omission of combative thinking. When you have great people around instructing you, it is very important to make sure that you have some type of advantage over them that will make it impossible for them to make it without you. In comparison being the brilliant one, if you often downplay the brilliance within you then you will be able to see all those pitfalls ahead and the perks of not having the people around you know all your full capabilities.

Jewel 39. When a woman gets between the man and his money, then she can rest assure she has the mind. The common knowledge of how a man loves his money is a great way to judge the authenticity of this jewel. I as a man can relate to the closest thing that a man or an individual can sometimes be with is his money even though sometimes it will let him down. The woman usually gauges the control she has over a man by attempts at his last amount of money.

Jewel 40. A person appearance is relevant to her immediate environment, but not pressingly important; before casting final Judgement, allow it to depend on how well she thinks. It is a strange thing to see someone in a rough neighborhood with a suit and tie on. It will not register to the individual all of what the person might be, rather an attorney, preacher or a Federal officer, or CIA agent. It would not strike anyone of this person that he was a success, and this is the image of this person. So, it the same with anything, but also with a woman she may appear to dress, skimpy or very formal but look inside her mind and see what it is that is so amazing about her or so daunting.

Jewel 41. If you have someone close to you that can be used and from time to time, they mutually use you, then this is a great relationship. When you or that individual can no longer be used; then you become useless. Otherwise what are friends for? The one thing friends are for is to be able to trade certain services that may or may not be able to be obtained by just any random individual. Friends are always supposed to be there for each other and be able to respect this relationship that has an unconditional love and camaraderie that goes beyond each other flaws and imperfections. The few true friends that I have I love them despite that one or two may be horrible people and therefore it's impossible for us to really get together often as we would like.

Jewel 42. Once the slaves won their freedom, they lost their purpose, and sense of direction after the war. This new freedom led them to not knowing what to do. Some found their way back to the cotton fields and watermelon patches. Our destiny doesn't

lie within the walls of prison nor the tobacco fields. Our freedom is a great responsibility to our people. Our destiny lies in the leadership of this great nation. W.E.B Du Bois, quoted that Before the Civil War, the Negro was certainly as efficient a workman as the raw immigrant from Ireland or Germany. But whereas the Irishmen found economic opportunity wide and daily growing wider, the Negro found public opinion determined to' Keep him in his place'. In addition, I think that it is wise to note that he also quoted, "North as well as South, the Negros have emerged from slavery into serfdom of poverty and restricted rights. All of that was said to say this, we must have a purpose in mind and if we don't then we as a people will fall into obscurity and oblivion only to spend generations upon generations of lifetimes to resurrect the dreams of others.

Jewel 43. Prejudice never shows much reason nor racism any sense, and discrimination will always be the inheritance of another person ignorance. It is my philosophy that when the wealthy whites pass down their riches then they are no longer concerned with the foolishness of skin color, but when the poor whites have nothing to pass on and there is no physical inheritance then racism will have to do. It was once spoke on a comedy show, asking a man that was obviously what we call in this generation a straw boss or a house negro. This negro had more riches then the rest of the other negros, so he felt privileged to be in this place and felt a sense of loyalty to those that he felt allowed him to exist there. Then he was asked did he believe racism still existed in America, His very answer was with the connotation of a slave with his eyes held down and a very humble response saying No Sir. And even if it is, I haven't seen none. There is no excuse to act in a manner of racism with today's knowledge of how foolish it is

Jewel 44. To Just a wake up one morning and say I'm going to change today is next to impossible. Behavior can be put under controls for a period and when the controls are removed in all the efforts that comes with change; the individual will most certainly revert to the way that seems most comfortable. Except some horrific, overwhelming, and life threating event happens to motivate a change, then it won't be possible to choose to change or not. This is the very thing that people face with health issues. Either they are faced with stop smoking, drinking lose weight, or the consequences is surely death. Even when people come home from prison the transition is never that simple to change over to an honest life if the practice of correction has not been put in place during the time of incarceration. The truth of the matter is not only do some inmates released come home worst then they were before they went in but also those that try to lose weight smoke and drink become worst after the veil attempt to stop. It is my honest opinion that in the success of mostly anything the change is long and bitter. It's processed in the mind and fought over before it is brought out into the physical. Then the fight only gets worst as it is practiced, but the fight is over time won with small victories that only the individual may know about and what seem like to the rest of us as quitting something cold turkey is a long road of being sick and tired of being sick and tired. And then there's the car accident near death experience but that's another Jewel.

Jewel 45. Freedom is a luxury that people have, but it has cost someone else dearly. History has proven time and time again that freedom comes only at the price of bloodshed. Every war, uprising or revolt in the history of every nation has come with two words, Freedom and Bloodshed. Someone wants the freedom of financial, religious, or civil and are willing to die for it. It was Patrick Henry that said Give me liberty or give me death at a speech he made to the second Virginia Convention on March 23, 1775 at St. John's Church in Richmond, Virginia. Some people find true freedom is only found in death and therefore bloodshed is inevitable when it's time to choose.

Jewel 46. Those who do not attempt to conquer themselves and master self-control are twice defeated. Their environment will overwhelm them 1ˢᵗ then the battle with in will shake their foundation, leave them defenseless; lastly overtaking them. To know thy self is to master yourself and to conquer thoughts and tendencies that don't represent who you have come to accept who you are. The journey in the mind must be made first of discovery. Because if not then the environment that one lives in will expose certain weaknesses about us and then we will be forcing to act with sense of moral values, purpose or inner sense of direction. When you know who you are, it will be very difficult for someone else to convince you otherwise.

Jewel 47. When getting into your car to thump your music going nowhere in the hood. It is best to stay clear of pedestrians you know who will want a ride to also go nowhere. This will become an expensive habit carrying two people around with nowhere to go but want to go everywhere. Don't open these doors unless it's necessary for travel, when having a car walk or ride a bicycle. It is more expensive to ride around one individual going nowhere fast than two. Therefore, it is better to have a clear destination and a time frame to have everything done, in these early stage time machines that we call cars. I used to always have someone throwing up their hand at me when I rode by and when I did, they would poke their head in the car and ask either which way was I going, or could they catch me up the street. This was a dangerous way to use this vehicle because now their purpose and all the results negative or positive trumped what I had going on and left me looking at what I could have gotten done in the rearview. The fact of the matter is that since I didn't have anything going on, they could read that message across my forehead and could asking in a way that almost had them grabbing the door handle to open the door before I could tell them to get in. When a man is determined and set for a certain destination, most people walking will rather walk than to have you ride them around 50 thousand places passing all the places that they could stop and further their agenda when all they had to do was walk a little further down the street.

Jewel 48. Man is most alive when he is closest to death. This is also when a man is the most honest. He will tell the truth about things that would have had him live with a destroyed life if he was going to have to live with long term regrets of the truth but because perhaps, she was on her way out then the truth has set her free. In addition, the man becomes more of a risk taker furthermore having a brush with death will cause the individual to savor parts of life that he has been taking for granted. Jumping out of planes skydiving and spending money on luxuries is just a few examples. Near death experience almost always makes a man reflect on his life and urges him to either write a book or love the love of his life as if he wants her last memories of any man to be him.

Chloe

Lil Chloe, with your stretched-out arms,
screaming quick someone hold me.

Then once lifted as the Angel you are, it's
fascinating to watch you grow

And boldly, pointing that curious lil finger
wanting to touch everything you see

One day you'll have to show papa all the
things that you came to know

Your snagged tooth smile warms me like a
blanket in that day it's always cold

If I'm moving slowly to get to where you are
my little star who came from heaven

It's because you've run me ragged and I
can't keep up because I'm old

So precious as a lil girl on my knee at 11 to a woman
I rest my head on at 27 Dedicated to Chloe Joy

Jewel 49. If a man felt freedom was worth fighting for, he wouldn't sit back so comfortably, and let others fight for him. Instead he relaxes and continue being a slave. This is surely the great conundrum, Believing in something sometimes is bigger than yourself, and everyone don't believe the same so just to say that everyone around me doesn't feel as free as I do, yet they expect me to go out and fight their cause because it's believed that if the fight is won then the person will enjoy the benefits of the blood bath by new found freedom.

Jewel 50. It's time for women to start seeing things as they really are; and not what she would like it to be. It is time to analyze the reality of world we live in and not as we hope it to be. Some women are in relationships that they hope will get better, but because of the hazy cloud that hovers over them of living life happily ever after. This is the dream that they were sold and are committed to seeing it through. In another situation I've considered was sometimes a doctor must instill hope in a patient and love ones to perform certain surgeries. This is true to all kinds of fields such as psychology and religion. The pessimistic will see things in a different light then the optimistic person, so it all depends on what is really going on and being able to just see what is in front of you and analyze the situation.

Jewel 51. Never make the same mistake twice. This is my best assessment to an individual that makes the exact same mistake twice is that there is some insanity in the person mental. Doing the exact same thing and expecting different results is insane. It is like my life where I was convicted for a major crime that led me to 5 years in prison. I can never go through with that act again; I will see it afar off get nervous and turn around and go the other way. It is all about the failures of life and what is it that we are trying to achieve. Those that want to succeed will always push forward beyond the mistakes of the past and move forward toward the direction of prosperity and success.

Jewel 52. One must be cultivated in wisdom to be rich; To be poor anyone can manage. I want to be a million air anyone can say that but to commit to the act, is a commitment that will change your life forever. Jim Rohn said that becoming wealthy wasn't the complete act of just working hard getting money, but it would build character and work ethic. He quoted that it wasn't the millions of dollars that held the most value but what it would make you become to get it. This is his way of saying that the accumulated wisdom was very wealthy, and this was necessary for you to keep the money. There is so much to say about self-development in this area, because first you will have to have some type of accomplishment to prove to the world that you are worthy to be followed down this dark grim road of work and little play. The cultivation in wisdom is being emerged in the things that you are passionate about and holds the practices of excellence.

Jewel 53. The bigger you think the bigger you become. It was said of Ray Charles after his death that he thought big, and this is most likely the reason that he crossed so many boundaries during his lifetime in music. Lastly, whatever a man thinks and puts in his vision then he can accomplish it. His thoughts become his words and then his words will become his action, then his action will become his character, and then his character will become his destiny.

Jewel 54. When passion boils over, we are not clearly aware sometimes we still go ahead not fully knowing who is it that goes ahead in such a manner. If we can turn our thoughts down when this happens in the heat of the moment, we could learn from the mistake before it even occurred. The excellent philosophy for hindsight, which is basically having the discipline to not do what you feel emotionally that you want to do and then see the destruction that it may cause and learn from it. Why is it that we have all the time in the world to learn from a mistake that has already happened but have never put anything into place that will cause us to learn after the fact.

Jewel 55. Our body is a small universe, to regulate feelings and emotions in harmony, these two great universes should be a constant reminder how the true nature and order of things bring off set less than inches could be disastrous. This constant reminder of the universe is no coincidence of how our bodies alongside the galaxies and beyond share a similar force field that if working together that it will produce a system such as the solar system or the body's immune system has an order and discipline that must be carried out.

If worked in perfect formation, then it will keep on track with the many orbits that are conjoined with it and it will work in perfect order.

Jewel 56. Even though being deceived by people is awful, it is better for that, then to always be on the lookout for deception. This is to keep one safe from paranoia. Neither should one have intentions to harm another, even though it is best to have to harm one to stay safe, then to lack the awareness to avoid being harmed, by others. This is to keep you from being careless, if one can keep both sayings in mind, one can be precise yet friendly. It is to my best understanding, that we have suspicions and rightfully so. It is unfortunately that we must be watchful in our moment in time now. It is not healthy to always look for someone to get us or be had. It must walk the earth with the intelligence of the signs of the gotten and what situations that we need to stay away from that may be scams or con artist. While no one wants to be on the other end, being the scammer or the con artist, but we must have a certain knowledge of what they know to keep from being a victim. This is the truth and principles of all laws, to know them front and backwards so that way when you see the fraudulent that you can be leery and get away from the gut feeling bad situation.

Jewel 57. People deceptions are not always revealed in words, when you notice this and show no change of attitude towards this person, your advantage over them can be endless. People sometimes wear their feelings on their sleeve for the world to see. Yet at the same time the visible outburst of emotions tells so much of how you think of people actions, and how it affects you. If a person wrongs, you and think they all the time have you at a disadvantage and you are all the time aware of this then it is you that have the advantage and able to cash in on this ignorance at first opportunity.

Jewel 58. Human life last only a hundred years at the most and the average life is between 60-75. These few days slip away as a sexual climax in the enjoyment of them. Those who would live happily know the abundant day of having life and remember the sorrows of wasting it. The value of life is precious, which the greatest resource that we have is time. It often goes unnoticed to the user and as drugs or alcohol. Gulped up and swallowed in large amounts, yet in vain because it is not consumed with the power or the intent to use this energy for life to change the world. It is so much that can be done in one day. In fact, it should be with a small amount of grief that the day is ending because you weren't able to do all that you could in that day.

Jewel 59. The deterioration in old age are caused during one's youth, the woes of ones declining years are created during ones prime. Therefore, people should be mindful how they eat, drink, and exercise in early years. This is an ongoing struggle that as Americans especially we battle with. We consume massive amounts of alcohol, smoke cigarettes and eat without questioning of the protein, cholesterol or fats. And exercise is almost out the question, but as I complete the description of this Jewel I'm committing to more exercise.

Jewel 60. Whatever good you've done to a person, throw it in the sea of forgetfulness, think about what better you can do. Also, be concerned with if you have offended anyone. Don't forget what others have done for you and forgive what others have done to offend you. It is expedient that we hurry to forget the good that we do to an individual because it is so easy to get stuck and dwell on something that has happened and now can do no longer do you any good. The equation to this mathematical problem is that when people do us wrong that we should quickly get over it and move on, but when we offend someone then we should make matters better by resolving the issue as quickly as we can.

Jewel 61. If you are in a haste that people know that you've done something good, then there is bad in your good. If you are afraid that people will find out if you've done something bad, then there is good in bad. This to me is the simple element of life in terms of, you know what you did. What feels right most of the time is and you can feel when you've done something bad. What we must understand is that we can't go out of the way to let people know what we have done something good like give someone a large sum of money. This is the arrogance of man and is very deceptive. And if we have done something that we are ashamed of is good for the conscious like smoke crack then this is genuine and may not do it anymore.

Jewel 62. Just by a person living risk sorrows. There's nothing to prevent mistakes or guarantees success entirely. All we can do is use all the information we have at the time to make decisions, then live, listen, and learn. We can live as cautiously as we can, but murphy law is still waiting with his head raised high as if providence was on his side. The risk comes with living in this day and time and what we must consider is what we know at the time of our living. It is so much that has changed from a hundred years prior, and the falsehood of what we thought was true in our living is null and void. For an example learning that Christopher Columbus didn't discover America, or all blacks didn't come from nations with bones in their noses, rather some were richer than the masters that they went to serve. And the Land of America which named After Amerigo Van Pucci was known already by so many great nations, but by the self-centered Englishman at the time thought they were the only ones that existed in the world that this was all new to them in discovery.

Jewel 63. What hell we put ourselves through to find heaven and its right before our very eyes all the time. Langston Hughes wrote a poem that went Life for me ant been no crystal stair, it has tacks in it. Boards torn up, places no carpet on the floor bare. But all the time I's been climbing on. Reaching landings, turning corners and sometimes going in the dark where their ant been no light. So, don't you stop, don't you set down on those steps now, because you find it's a kind of hard. I's still going, I's still climbing. This poem was a single mother telling her son of the struggles of life and that no matter what he must persevere on. If you can't fly as an eagle, run like a lion, if you can't run like a lion walk like a man, if you can't walk like a man, crawl like the spirit of God once it is upon you to eventually change the world forever. We produce our own scenarios and visions of life, how we interpreted it and respond to it. Yet we put ourselves in these terrible positions trying to find the good in life and just by living, just by being enclosed in our right mind, just by being able to leave a nugget of jewel with you at this moment as I typed I've reached heaven and understand that it doesn't have to wait after death to come down from the sky. Living, breathing and being coherent is heaven enough.

Jewel 64. Can a person call back again the words that have left their mouth to be silent? Therefore, think carefully before you respond to an asked question. One may get the wrong impression or take offense. The effects could be detrimental. This is the great conundrum that lies in journalism. Trying to find out what it is that the athlete or movie star or whoever the world is at the time so intrigued with and get an honest answer. It is possible that those people want to give you an honest answer that may have even stemmed from an opinion, but because that narrative of the story may not be as exciting as the world may have hoped for, then the journalist may have to spruce the story up a bit and even be subjective or objective to the story. Therefore, PR's are needed to get as much of the real you out without being put in a compromising position. We know that we must watch our thoughts, they become words, watch our words they become actions, watch your actions, they become habit, watch your habits they become your character, watch your character they become your destiny.—written by Lao Tzu.

Sometimes it's great to practice a moment of silence to give yourself the time to answer questions that you might not fully understand or have complete knowledge of. It will save you embarrassment and headache in the long run. With care we must guard what we feel and anticipate the bloopers and blunders of misunderstanding. So, when explaining something as if a person was slow to understand, I state the well-known misconceptions that what my answers are is not. Then with clarity what it is and be clear again in closing what it is not so that no matter what information they gathered that they may try to use against me because he said one thing then said something else, it will always be he said one thing, said something else, and then said what he said at first again, so what he said at first must be true.

Jewel 66. A man who spends time biting his fingernails is an idle man, He may be in a hurry to get an important task done but has become immobilized and idle with nothing more to do

than eat away at his own flesh and consume germs. When this man becomes busy enough to think about things, he hasn't done yet and must do. He won't have time to bite at his hand nor think about it. Those hands will be too busy doing the things it needs to do.

I was just about to bite my fingernails while lost in thought about a speech I'm preparing, homework for my degree in my masters that I'm obtaining and a family crisis all at the same time. Then I realized in thought I was idle and was about to bite my fingernails. Then I realized that I must continue and keep typing. We are so often in thought about something that we can't do anything about right now. Then the only action that we can take is to bite our nails and wonder on and not get anything done physical.

Jewel 67. Even though a situation may need immediate attention, never be in such an impulsive hurry where you don't have all the accurate information to act accordingly. To move slower and precise may be better than quickly and ignorantly in error. This is the good quality that all leaders have. It is being able to gather information and process it, and even being able to account for not having all the information to make the right decision. It is a gift and not a skilled learned because so many people act erratic and out of emotion. The purpose of giving yourself the time to move slower than normal is because once you act, then it's impossible sometimes to go back and have a do over decision.

Jewel 68. Don't be led to believe what people say about someone to change your personal views of them; but don't reject their words entirely either. Use what you see, know, and with a little common sense to form the reality. Your views of a person are your views and should not be influenced by someone too much. If someone tells me something about a person, I always ask a few questions and then see for yourself what the person is doing and how does the information identify with the person.

Jewel 69. When your mind is full of ignorance, it's hard to even focus on filling it with fruitful knowledge of Jewels. One must have clear mind to enhance learning skills; and willingness to reach towards knowledge that may take digging to obtain. It is such a shame that some people have so much rage, negativity, and misery in their mind that it's impossible for them to see the good and the positive that is right in front of them. They suffer from mild or acute mental illnesses and ignorance is the only right that they know. It is quite a shame that even with knowledge in front of them that they are bewildered and baffled from this information and after no reason will turn around and look for any other information to prove their thinking right, because this is what is safe and for them positive. The garbage of their own thoughts is the wealth of knowledge that they are happiest with and refuses to listen unless it comes from a source of foolishness.

Jewel 70. Happiness is pursued through hardship and struggle, if ever obtained, there's very little that can take it away, and hard times have already been overcame. This a Jewel that lets us know that it is fitting to go through hell to get to heaven. In fact, that is the only way to appreciate it. It is the only way to be able to recognize that all that we have accomplished, is worth it and can then be properly synthesized.

Jewel 71. If what you say 95% of the time, is right, you will not necessarily be praised for it. If 9 out of 10 plans workout, you will not necessarily be looked upon as an accomplished planner. But when one's plan fails, or a single mistake is made. Everyone will blame you and put great emphasis on these errors, as if it was your destiny to fail. If failures not an option, calculate a little under what you expect so you'll have cushion to fall within target. It's better to be beyond your goal, then to fall short. This is true in so many levels of life when it comes to why we fail as individuals. It is customary that we challenge ourselves as humans to accomplish so great feat, so we set the stakes high, we get others involved so that we can have others to help hold us accountable. But then we fail, we miss the mark, we lose sight of our vision, we forget all the steps we planned to be successful and then we error. Not knowing that when this happens all that was with us, dreaming with us, and putting the work will now go overboard. The old saying goes that you can't do the exact same thing and expect different results, this is insanity. The mistakes that we make in the past should be buried and the accomplishments that we make should be made aware to all around us to let them know that it is possible.

Jewel 72. You must take pride in your own beauty or if you are handsome, because if you don't consider your own looks, then who will. However, in beauty there is hidden ugliness, and in handsome there is the hideous. Search for purity and your outer appearance within will glow. The only one true beauty is the one within, because the outer appearance is always changing and failing. The handsome man must be pure in thought to have true mannerism that glows without, and beauty must be purified within to outlast the natural skin showing radiance in her eyes and her child like smile will be magnificent.

Jewel 73. When a man pride is on the line, and he's pushed in a corner, he's worse than a cat clawing his way out. But more like a rat when he's infringed upon. He will lie and cheat, chewing his way out with violence. It is said in the bible that it was pride that caused Lucifer to fall, and pride also is one of the seven deadly sins. Man has only his name and honor in our time of living that is of true value and the pride of that will cause him to an early death if he is not careful. To my best knowledge most of my most severe mistakes was because of pride and not wanting to look like I was weak, soft, or unable to complete the lifelong task of being a man.

Jewel 74. Comfort peoples when they make mistakes, share in their troubles, dare not to intrude on their success, if not invited, this will lead to resentment. Life has a funny way of putting you in people lives, some for a lifetime other for only a moment. The reasons why sometime never fully known, but what is clear is that we suppose to comfort those individuals when mistakes are made and not look down on them. Likewise, when the successes are achieved then it must be an invitation sent to come in to celebrate with them. This may not seem like its fair, but it's just life.

Jewel 75. If at first you find it hard to part ways with bad people, refrain from criticizing them. This will cause animosity, and trouble will be made for you. If you are not able to enter the presence of good people and live in it, don't praise them from afar. People will notice and begin to slander them. The one thing that everyone loves are praises and it is criticism that helps the individual if it is constructive. The negative people that we surround ourselves with at times are not worth trying to criticize. In fact, it is better to leave them alone and let them have at their own lives. A lot of people plug in headphone to their listening devices such as cell phone and keep a conversation going or music to block out the world or to create a sense of reality that you're not there. Good people have a tendency of getting a bad rap. I'm sure you've have heard the saying that she thinks she or he is better than me and that this person or that person is stuck up and you will have to be challenged to find something good to say about them. So instead of doing so where others may hear and wonder what is truly the nature of the person that you speak of then it must be up close and personal. This way they notice and can be modest and share praises with others. Too kind Too Kind.

Jewel 76. A religious man out of fearfulness of the wrath of God to come; worships and gives from his finance to the different faces of faith. A man who has no religion also worships and gives of his finances. However, his is done all towards things in the world, with no fear. It's best a man does things out of love than fear. When man is motivated to act it is because he loves his self or fear what may happen if he does not act. There are times when men are forced to be motivated by others such as loved one. It is similar with the acts that motivate those that give money in the name of faith. It is caused at times because he simply wants to find his place in the kingdom of God. While others do it because it makes financial sense to donate to charitable organizations for returns and taxes benefits at the end of the year and makes them sleep better at night.

Jewel 77. When you must compromise to make others happy; only that is not a good compromise. The best compromise is when no one gets entirely what they want. This is the definition of compromise to both be mostly satisfied, and yet not entirely upset. A lot of people never get the concept of compromise. While some think the compromise is you give up what you are, where you are in life, who you are in life then the compromise is selfish. Both parties should be able to interpret what compromise is and then act on it.

Jewel 78. He who cannot think cannot survive. The idea of thinking is for complete survival. Mankind has not ascended to its highest heights because of our reasoning and our lack of thinking. Why we don't spend more time thinking and meditation is astounding. The more we think and more focus we are then we will ascend to higher heights. We will survive.

Jewel 79. When one is constantly in search for resolution, even in the smallest matters, never hypocritical towards others to salvage friendship, and not reckless with speech. This is a hero brought forth. The selfless acts of an individual are the characteristics of a hero. When a person operating in their gift and from their heart has made a commitment to excellence and doing all that they can to produce results.

Jewel 80. Much wealth can never bring divine happiness nor add joy, but a small favor can cause endless gratitude. My mentor Lynn Claiborne has spent with me the greatest resource known to mankind, which is time. I have told her many times that I am very appreciative of the time that she has spent to make me a better speaker. She has in return told me that she believes in me and that she has also felt that her time was well spent and that she was appreciative of my sincere will to learn from her. She spent money on some out of the country liquor, I'm sure it will be gone soon, When I become successful, I will drink it in celebration of her belief in me. Money is something that I know isn't everything, and it doesn't solve all the problems, but people will quickly say that they want to see for themselves.

Jewel 81. When there is trouble among anyone, one should remain calm and not get excited, when your closest friends are in error, one should be stern and not push the situation aside. This is the catch twenty-two, in terms of allowing people to push your buttons yet at the same time being able to respond in a manner that is mature and responsible. It was just today that I allowed someone to get me out of my character. We spoke of high values of being men and demanding respect, but we argued like children and acted as if we were going to fight like fools. In the mist of keeping calm it is important to use other jewels like being able to learn from the mistake before making it and exercising patience. I did not remain calm and I didn't exercise patience. With the two people that I had the altercation with were friends and people work with. The bible lets us know that we should be careful of arguing with people because afar it is difficult to determine who the fool is. I mentioned it to my brother, and he wasn't ready to hear this truth now. He apologized and so did I, and by gone were by gone. Neither one pushed the situation aside and by being stern we understood the lesson of how to talk to each other with a level of respect.

Jewel 82. A person is constantly leaking life from the day they were born. The most important responsibility for one who knows this is not to repair the leak, but to do all he/she can with the life while it's yet still contained. It is better to live a full happy life and die at 35 then to have a life of safety and somewhat meaningless with little adventure or happiness at 100. While some look for a life safe in the corner, three meals a day and a blanket to keep them warm, it is some destiny to have a life of uncertainty, adventure, risk, and the scare of experiencing life because you're not going to make it out alive.

Jewel 83. Many worries are a great misfortune, and to have concerns are a great fortune. Those left in despair over many concerns fully know of less worries; and those who live life in peace of mind fully knows the suffering of many worries. It is my guess in this jewel that experience is perhaps a teacher, not necessarily the best teacher. But when those know of the pain of a certain situation or position to be in then they tend not to never forget it. It is also worth noting that when people tend to do very well in life that they don't know of the worries of the situation. So, their experience has not delivered them to a life that has traumatized them which allows them not knowing of the concerns that are before them to escape the suffering.

Dedicated to Stacy

Goddess

It took me a thousand years to get here
To hold you close and become one flesh and one bone
And when you held me close
Ever since then you've been right here, right by me
Goddess
Baby breath are in your eyes
And the roses
Is right here beside me
It just took a thousand years it was, worth a thousand years.
This weather makes me want to make love, love you in the rain
Stroke your body with my fingers as a
brush and your body is the
Canvas to my new masterpiece.
Opening you up like the gift that you are and
spread you on the bed as red roses
Your perfect proportion of your naked body lying
there is like poetry's proses and sonnets.
Your rhythm catches aptitude and raises me higher
with every word you whisper in my ear
You are the enchanting Goddess sent to me,
to keep me focus and ever clear

By: Marvin Thomas

Jewel 84. When the disease of Aids sets into the immune system it breaks down. Rapid weight loss and sickness will occur. Therefore, for one who seeks to live on a higher level. Should not wish to rid themselves of obvious faults when hidden faults still exist. Simply put there is a hidden world of wants and desires that will affect you one way or the other. Such as Lupus, cancer and other diseases of the body, one tends to move along with the aspiration of living in a higher plane of life when there are so many things that will tear you apart from the inside. It is best that we first focus on the things that will tear us apart from the inside even though it will hinder your upward movement for the moment.

Jewel 85. The bequest of our ancestors is what we are enjoying now. The welfare of our descendants is what we currently leave; both are hard to build up and very easy to lose or throw away. What we do with our lives not only affect the lives of those that are around us now, but it affects those that are not even born yet. Maybe even hundreds of years down the road. In addition, it is the same legacy that those before us have left, worked hard for and sacrificed, which are the enjoyments of our well-being. To say the least in this matter the benefactors of what we enjoy and the freedoms that we experience, are all because of what someone else has done previously.

Jewel 86. To be quiet and calm are two different things, one can be very angry and yet quiet, but he has not kept calm. To be calm in the midst of activity is a true state of patience. This is a practice that many must perfect in such a gift to be quite when the time comes. It has been my experience up to this very moment where someone has come up against my family and spoke against it with division. I must be calm and handle the situation with grace. The purpose of not allowing the situation to understand the anger in your life is because it will be a determining factor of the total outcome. Yet if the environment doesn't know the anger that resides on the inside then you have the leverage and the advantage.

Jewel 87. A playgirl can become a good wife in her later years and her early indiscretions are no more thought about. A chaste wife can lose her virtue in later years and all her former purity

becomes forgotten. It is true that we so easily forget, and people do change. Yet when a woman has put herself in a mode where she finds that her freedom is in the chances she takes with strong drink, men or even drugs then this course must play itself out. No man on the earth can change this mind set. It must be matured and grew out of her. Then after she has made all her mistakes and realizes mortality and time that will catch her in mid stride of putting on her lip stick and she notices the wrinkles on her lips only then will she feel a little bit better of catching the man of her dreams. All will be forgotten, and she will be the best wife that a man could ever stumble across not even expecting her history of indiscretion. The exact same with the chaste wife that has done well so long in life and all has come to know and respect. Then one slips up in later years and society will judge her as a woman that should have known better and gotten that foolishness out of her system.

Jewel 88. To regret past errors is not as good as preventing future mistakes. Preserving priorities or goals already accomplished is never as good as to count on success not yet attained. This Jewel used correctly will make someone very successful because it is the past mistakes that hold people back and yet it is also the same mistake that pushes that individual over the edge knowing that they don't have the time or luxury to continue making mistakes such as the one that they could spend too much time regretting. It also to no avail to find confront in what you have accomplished because it will be the grave of you. We must never become stagnate. Movement towards what has not happened yet, but the constant preparation for when it does that you can be successful.

Jewel 89. When your thoughts are perfectly clear you see the realness of substance in mind. So, you should always relax and keep calm, and allow your mind to remain upbeat. Nothing gives more leisure to a person than a peace of mind. This is the silhouette of success when you have a clear mind and perspective. Clarity is the cornerstone builders' block of success by giving you the focus you need to obtain your goals. We must emerge in this relax and calm state with the focus to want to conquer the world. To dominate and have no competition to bother us on our way to completion of our objectives. The belief that this is already in our power to do so gives us the mindset of peace.

Jewel 90. It may not be fully known how cheap a house is if kept clean, or how poor a young girl is if she's well-groomed and dressed. If one was to fall on hardship and their appearance is well kept, no one will know or be able to judge. I have gotten into many circles of champions by dressing the part and looking the part and acting the part. The truth is that around some of these smart, wealthy and powerful people that I set at the table and took interest in their business model, I had got dropped off because I didn't own a car. I was poor with no money and had no idea how I would continue a relationship that looked as if I could meet these people somewhere and pay my own way. Yet I learned that if dressed well enough and groomed well enough that my actions could get me into doors that I may not have been accepted or respected in. A house similar would be looked at as not necessarily expensive but neither cheap if the yard is cut and great furniture.

Jewel 91. When thoughts rear its ugly head to full fil its desires, quickly one must grab its head and direct it towards reason. This could mean the difference between calamity and good fortune, or life and death. The desires of an ugly thought, most of the time has its own selfish agenda. The plan or purpose of the individual must be in focus to direct the thought to reason. This is the square or the straight and narrow road that is written about in the bible and other various books that pushes us to believe that when a person wonders off the charted course of his previously pinpointed destination then he must return to the voice of reason.

Jewel 92. Sometimes a vessel will tip over when it is full. When full piggy banks are often broken into on purpose, yet when it's empty it remains whole. Seek to contain Jewels but give them to those in need. If not when the time come when seekers of knowledge come to you, they'll break you into pieces. This is a powerful way to look at that which is within a person must be distributed out accordingly. In fact, it must be done with such discretion that it will run some of the seekers away when it is ask of them the requirements of what it takes to get something from within.

If you have information that a person seeks, don't be so readily to expose or give up the information so easily. This is something that you had to obtain by either a network, by some means of effort or cost. Then people not even realizing the true worth of what it is that they ask, will nonchalantly ask you to give up to them what you may have worked so hard for. Therefore, you must always appear empty, because you will not have the individual coming to you asking for free what is more valuable than they can obtain nor, would they know what to do with it if handed over. Also, it is those people that see you full and think this is a great weight for you to have upon your shoulders and would rather break you into pieces than to ask for mentorship or advice on how they could gain such fullness.

My Rootz

It was not long ago that I prepared a speech called rootz to I am, and it started with a poem by Langston Hughes as such. Life for me haven't been no crystal stare it has tacks in it. Boards torn up places with no carpet on the floor bare. But all the times I've still been climbing on. Turning corners, reaching landings and sometimes even going in the dark where there an't even been no light. So, don't you stop now, don't you sit down on those steps because you find it kinds a hard. I still going, I still climbing.

This was the poem that I used, and I felt it appropriate to use in my speech rootz to I am because this poem in fact was a single mother talking to her son trying to inspire him through all the hardships that he may face in life that he can't stop, he must keep going. From Moorish Spain of 711 to 1492 through slavery and the civil rights area, to the injustices we face in police brutality and senseless murders by cops we must continue. It is in my generation that we have experienced such nonsense as to die early and young. Mass incarceration were 1/3 blacks are in prison or in engaged in Department of Justice system. It is the same ration of young black males under 21 will likely be killed prematurely. When I met Nikki Giovanni, I showed her my books that I wrote and the poems that I dedicated to her. She was somewhat moved but not impressed to the point that she wanted to meet with me right away and discuss my goals and endeavors that I had planned. It was only after I called and told her that I have been enriching myself into toastmasters that she said that she would give me advice and the help that I needed to pursue my goals. I would like to take a moment to thank LaKeshia Whitehurst and Cori Fonville, for inviting me to Toastmasters, it has drastically changed my life forever.

Jewel 93. If someone has made a mistake that you need to address. Do not become enraged with anger. After you've calmed down; even if it's something hard to say, do not hint indirectly calmly address it directly and do not push any issue aside lightly. This is the indecisiveness that we face daily. People offend us, and they will do it again if we don't come to them and correct them, or at the very least let them know how we are offended. Now it is within our power to let people know in our environment that they cannot exist there with a mindset. Keep negative and garbage out of conversations that are delivered to you. And when you have a problem with a person instead of being fake and no genuine approach the individual and with a non-threating mindset, let the individual know how you feel about them.

Jewel 94. To criticize people for minor faults do not mean that they are major mistake makers or often found in slip ups. It only means that they're highly watch. My assessment to this observation is that if you look for small details in a person action that determines that they made a mistake you are watching them way to close and for what purpose? Some watch because they are trying to reduce the imagist of failure in their own mind of their lives.

Jewel 95. A solitary perfectionist can do the world no good. Such a person must interact with people, so they can benefit from them. To remove themselves from the equation is like removing manure from soil or salt from water, which neither could bore no crop or freshwater fish. Some purities can do nothing alone without its counterpart. It like the reproduction of humans, the male and the female must come together in order to have a baby. Even though science has almost phased out the natural process and only left the necessary function of the sperm and the egg to be fertilized. The birth of a child can now be done through a simple procedure, but during the time of this writing of this book, a male sperm is still needed. This is also, a great opportunity to bring up the value of networking. It is said that network is net worth. Jim Rohn said simply put that we must get around the right people. My picture of networking in my head is the picture of the Vitruvian man.

Jewel 96. It has been said, "It is no disgrace to have many afflictions; I would worry if there never were any afflictions". Slow progress is better than none, as sometimes it's difficult to tame a wild animal or to mold certain metals, but not impossible. As the growth of the Republic it is stated that Abraham Lincoln said that when the dreaming stop so does the Republic. The United States utilize the political process called congress, which goes back and forth, of different legislations. It was never meant to move forward fast, but to slowly move along with the growth of the people. If you are not trying hard to accomplish anything the chances are you want to have much backlash or opposition placed upon you.

Jewel 97. Strength can easily be turned into weakness by a little selfishness and greed, then knowledge into foolishness, then compassion into cruelty. A person's character can unfold into distinguished in one act, and crumble into nothing in another. This key gives us a deeper appreciation and revelation of the worth of our work. Sometimes we have good intentions of what we must do, the opportunity of a lifetime. Yet the thin line that exist in between the one-minute mark that determines whether you are early or late. It is a small room for error in the development of an individual that pushes to obtain a goal and allow short cuts and people he could sacrifice in order to get a dream or goal accomplished.

Jewel 99. One who has power must know how to make peace and to make war. This key should be referenced by all that is in power, and the importance here is detrimental to more than the person that is in authority. It is detrimental perhaps to people that are not even born yet, coming up in the area of when that decision was made. There is a certain burden that is held on the shoulders of those in power and used unwisely it could be the burden of those under the power of this individual.

Jewel 100. Prison is a place where some are birth into the world. Before being incarcerated, they had no credentials, work

history, or any trackable records to determine if they were a part of society. Until the experience of prison, then were their eyes opened and could see the true value of being productive and contributing to society. The one thing that I've seen personally in prison, from different cultures and backgrounds had similar stories. From the drug dealer to the individual that spent most of his young age robbing and stealing from people. They would find themselves almost at lost that they have never really involved themselves with the most intrinsic parts of society like having skills or a trade, a job and participation in the educational programs. This new wild journey that some of them take leads to life changing moments, others realize that they were better criminals and continue a life of crime, in terms of attempting to get smarter or wiser in the world of crime. After the completion of programs some I've seen want to go on and get their licenses upon release, and a social security card. Pushing the envelope and wanting to get a trade and good at something that they may provide themselves a life where criminal activity becomes null and void. Lastly, I want to say on this issue that is deeper than the ocean that, most people have never felt the effects of a functional society, how it works, and when you don't contribute to it, then there is a further price to pay. You can't borrow from a person and don't pay them back like in society, it may cost you your life. If you don't go to work you really want to eat, because the food that is served is so much of a low discounted brand that it is only consumable to those who become animals and refuse to walk upright as men. Disrespect never goes over the head of an individual without the risk of retaliation. This world for those that are lucky enough to make it out of, as I have seen the effects of those that want to be free and those that look at prison life and say I can live with that.

Jewel 101. It has been said people should not do more than one thing at a time; However, it's a new day in age now, when we must think and act in multiplicity. In doing many tasks at once, each one must be done in sequence with flawless execution, efficient in time management, and if delegation is necessary it must be done effectively. This is my favorite jewel that is why I saved it for jewel 101. As a dominate force that will activate greatness in the lives of those that practice such habits will inevitably become successful. It takes too much time to do everything one at a time, operating in singularity. Now I am writing this book I am also waiting on customers at Aroma City and listening to Dr. Myles Munroe audio for my self-development. Every now and then I squeeze my wife as she walks past to fill in the gaps of the time that I lose when I'm doing other things and my spoiled wife loves when I give her majority of my attention. Rule of thumb always have enough done so that when your wife challenges you by a seductive smile and a set down on your lap that you can drop what you are doing and give her your undivided attention. (Just saying)

Jewel 102. Physical healing cannot come except one has sought to heal the element of the minds, spirits, and soul. Only then can the body be free of impurities that causes physical sickness. Healing is a divine resolution. This is my true belief of divinity that the body only replicate what the mind, spirit and soul is. We are what we put inside our bodies and studies show of happy people that are married live longer on average than those that are single with the cat. Or those that are spirit filled have a healthier life than those that practice no religion. Sometime depression falls on those that are empty in will but with positive reinforcements a person can accomplish much.

Jewel 103. When a man leaves prison, he must be ready at the ride from prison, up until he reaches back to his community to find strength in his weakness to overcome recidivism. When he has been fully planted into the soil of society with this mindset; then he can bloom. We can look at this from so many different angles in terms of the ride home from prison and what it consists of. The ride home is the lethal projector of where a person may end up in life. This is the area of opportunity where people can focus on everything they've been through since they were knocked down. This crucial ride home must be walked with calculated steps. It was a friend of mine that was released from prison. His name was "O". His steps where calculated but not for the better. He would flat out tell all of us as he was leaving that he was going back out to sale more drugs to get back on his feet. He only had a few months, back on a probation violation. It was shortly after his release that we found out that he was murdered. Only if he had made the changes that were necessary to live and be productive then he may have made it. "O" was shot in the head and this haunted me after I heard it, to allow the ride home to set in remember why I must be successful. It's necessary to put an imaginary gun to my head to do the right thing before someone else did.

Jewel 104. A person who does not take full advantage of education, to pass down to their children, make use of public office to change and better living conditions, and obtain financial stability to do good works; is as a person even if they live a hundred year is if they had never lived at all. In this jewel it must be looked at closely that everyone has a purpose and a responsibility in life to do their part and leave the remains of their contributions and not a debt.

Jewel 105. Those who teach but themselves do not practice what's been taught, are only orators and under the illusion of their own rhetoric. Many can point the way, but a true teacher must also be headed in the direction they point. The teacher and the salesman are in the same boat according to the product they are selling or trying to get someone to buy into. It will be very hard to get someone to buy into something that the individual who supposedly has bought into but find out that they don't have. I would never buy a product from someone that they refuse to use, and I don't see myself listening to advice from someone that don't take heed to what they advise themselves.

Jewel 106. Teen suicide may be out of our control, but not beyond our responsibility. When red flags show up underneath your nose; it's our moral obligation to report it to the proper authorities. Every parent wants to be the cool parent even if they must decide against it. It is probably one of the most common actions to try to leave a child or teenager be giving them their space so that they want to tell other kids at school that they have no life and hate you for it. It is my best guess in the provision made for teenagers that we even look over some of the crazy things they do in order to allow them individuality and let them be themselves. I say unto you now that we can't allow children to be left alone to their own devices and if they hate us then so be it, but they are not allowed to push parents out of their lives and say they have friends now, so they don't need mom or stepdad. Their life may just depend on it.

Jewel 107. To awake one day and realize that you got to get up and do something is good; but to continue to lay there and not take it a step further; its best you stayed asleep. Because when or if you do put forth any effort, it could be too late. This is the strange thing that I battled with for so long and I decided until I make this a Jewel and a life principle then I would always deal with my problems from afar and lay there in debate mode going in and out of sleep wondering do I get up and do something about my life or do I lay down and take it. If we don't make a conscious effort to do something, then life will turn on us and it will write a script out for us and say here is your part. You'll be like an extra, no significant role and quickly the years will pass on quickly, as the hungry earth foams at the mouth to gobble you up and digest you to the land of oblivion to be forgotten about forever.

Jewel 108. The universe is without sound and moves in silence; yet its energy never finds rest, even for a while. The sun and the moon are in constant motion to us, both day and night. Their light never changes nor does the tide ever cease. An enlighten person will have a strong sense of urgency when at leisure, and a mood of relaxation when at leisure, and a mood of relaxation when they're busy. Energy is always in motion, can't be created nor destroyed, and this vibration is the Genesis of life. The person who knows this and have the skills to act upon it will start his mornings early and try to keep his goals that he is trying to accomplish managed and obtainable throughout the day. With a steady had on the things that after accomplished will make you great it will give you the confidence to work in no panic rush but, with a delicate urgency that you are engaged and would like to complete the task as soon as possible. And in a frantic push to get it done, you know everything will be brought together in unison. Then confidence lies deeper, it's the assurance that everything that it is happening has already happened and from my point of view already over with. You become successful long before it is measured by money or the amount of people you've influenced. It happens the moment you awake to greatness and understand the things you must do for the universe to continue, with the energy that you will disperse into the universe.

Jewel 109. Life is forever delivering a series of unpredictable changes, some good that makes life enjoyable, other times bad to make life miserable. To know bad times are coming makes it easier to cope and prepare for it. Don't be afraid of this change, look for it when it comes and bear it. Simply put, the mystery of life states we don't know why bad things happen to good people. Yet at the same time it happens, and our only concern is how are we prepared to deal with it. Seeing it happen to others don't quite do us justice in the area of empathy, but it can always give us ideas how to cope. Show us what others done to get through a similar situation and give us confidence to win in the face of tragedy. When we are afraid of the coming of change then it can ultimately make it worst when the change is neither good nor bad. Yet when we see change as a necessary part of life then the outlook would be so much better, and we will be at peace.

Jewel 110. Let us hurry along to do what we must do so we can have time to do what we want. Timing is always of the essences, and we must learn how to manage our time. Priorities are going to be a big factor in time management and the accomplishments of getting set objectives done. We don't have the time or luxury to give in to time wasting habits when there are a lot of things that we claim we want that requires our immediate attention.

Jewel 111. Leave nothing to chance, double up on everything when possible and if by some strange event your ship begins to sink, you'll have so much extra to throw overboard that will float, it will be impossible to drown. This is the not going down with the ship mentality, it is surviving save yourself and hope you packed enough for everyone. The life demanding accessories that don't come free or in the beginning are so key to survival. Yet we must struggle and work so hard for it, because our very lives depend on it if something goes wrong. To name just a few are family and friends which would fall under your networking systems, an accumulated amount of wealth, for provisions of food clothing and shelter, and lastly knowledge and information, so you can interpret all that has to happen with what you have.

Jewel 112. Do not go after the riches that will pass away, but seek wealth that perish not, and its accumulation has no end. After reading this passage then you could get up and go to the refrigerator and eat a piece of chicken. The only differences are that the passages in this book you read will stick with you forever, the chicken is gone in 4 to 6 hours. Information and knowledge are the riches of this world that will amass much wealth and can never be stolen.

Jewel 113. Perfection should not always be a distant goal, but at some point, a present-day new standard to be held to; And those that within a set time do not measure up, should be held accountable. This is the future that many are not ready for now. The perfection I speak of for an example is to say a person do not lie. If the person lies, then he has been deemed a liar and can no more be looked at as an honest man. This is an extreme example, but it is necessary to practice perfection with perfection. You can no longer be perfect in such a small thing as telling a lie when you have the power over your own words till the day we die. It is so many things that we can be perfect at without looking so far down the road saying when the time is right years down the road, I will be perfect in refraining from alcohol or drugs. We have been passed away dead from the truth that from our early roots the lies of we have all the time in the world to get it right. This is not true, yet the practice allows us to divulge in life without the anxiety of having to push contributions and societal responsibility.

Jewel 114. Pass glory does not excuse present guilt. People always talk about what they use to do, and where they have been in life. This may have been a powerful statement at one time, but it no longer matters what was in the pass. People usually feel bad and have regretful thoughts of what they should be doing and then bring up what they have done to prove to themselves what they at least did to comfort themselves during a time of laziness and loss of purpose.

Jewel 115. A enlighten person can never be so poor that they cannot aide and assist a person; because they can always speak a powerful word in due season to awaken the deft, dumb, and blind. This is such a tragedy, because it's like a person know that they are in a cage and the door is not locked. Yet no attempt is made to get out of the cage because everything that you think you need is always in the cage, food, water, and things to play with. Yet the power of flight is outside the cage, friends and family and most importantly freedom.

Jewel 116. Human sentiments cause people to cling to others when they are hungry, and then drift off moments later when they are filled. Bringing their bags to those who are in a comfortable circumstance, and quickly pack up and abandon them when they see them fall on hard times. A person that has a loyal spirit will continue with a person especially in time of need. Some people address this problem as just life. We understand there are parasites, that will suck you dry, and leave you for dead. These are often the same people that claim to be your friend, but if you perish won't even go to your funeral. These fair weathers, Johnny come lately men in our lives that have made it known through so many actions and speech that this is who they are, it is the person fault that they heard and seen what they wanted to hear. It is far and few in between that people will walk through the hell fire with you. It is very significant that a person can struggle through with another individual, it shows not only dedication to be there through good times as well but also shows a sign of empathy that gives the person that they are going through the tough times with the value of true friendship and what is necessary to maintain it.

Jewel 117. To caution yourself around important people is wise, it shows that you are not heedless; To humble yourself in the presence of small people is powerful, it shows that you're not just a common bully. This practice is surely to for awareness. It is smart to make sure that you let people know that you know who you are, because in the end, people will respect that and when they come around you, they will make sure that they let people know who you are. It is common courtesy to shadow yourself In the presence of an individual that has the highlight reel upon him and when you are in the mist of those that think that you are God and you appear low and humble, they will respect the idea that you are a regular person underneath all of that greatness.

Jewel 118. You can tell who cares about you the most by who comes to visit you in the hospital first; some are running late

buying flowers. To simply put it, coming to the hospital to visit a person is never done out of formality. In fact, rushing down to let them know that you are there for them is the only reason a person should be there. To the let them know that you care and making sure that when their eyes open when they awake that you are the first person that they see. The formality that doesn't mean nothing to the individual that lies in the bed racked in pain is your hair or make up done, the roses and the balloons or how you are dressed. So many people are still trying to make the right impression all the way to the graveyard.

Jewel 119. Let people drink if they will, but do not despise them for all being intoxicated; nor do not be proud of being the only one who is sober. As one bound to both religion or Godlessness, both are captivated with this idea, and free in mind. The same can be said of those that are drunkards or practice sobriety. This is the resonation of the religious idea of being pure in mind, body and soul. The individual that doesn't drink believes this as well as the individual that wants to be healthy, fit and not wanting live in the best condition if they can. It is only by grace and mercy that some of us are not subjected to the madness of the drunkards and living a life of disconnection of society. The freedom of mind is reflected upon the belief of our actions that shows the most positive results. Such as if a person doesn't drink and he is able to hold on to a job now, or feels better in the body, or simply doesn't hurt his family through violence, and obtaining dui's.

Jewel 120. The pleasures of life are not found in the delicacies of foods or fine wine; some afterwards still experience unhappiness and complete loneliness. The flavor of intense experience is always short-lived, while those that enjoy eating beans and drinking water is a subtler experience and longer lasting with pleasure. The true pleasures of life are to enjoy the small things and take delight in the trivial things that most can't even see. When those small disciplines are enjoyed and deeply engaged in then there is nothing that will spoil the individual from living a life of happiness. Greatness lies in the depths of the small and what might seem meaningless things.

Jewel 121. Timing is everything, and like all skills must be developed and mastered; for example, sometimes to arrive to early is just as bad as arriving too late. The master of timing is a well-developed skill and a craft that is always overshadowed by those that try to make up for lost time and have the energy to compile time through overtime. Also, it is worth mentioning that if I'm on time then I am early awaiting the time to come. Being late is one minute after the time appointed to be there. If I had a speaking engagement in another state that was critical to my career, then I would most likely show up a day early so that way I won't worry about anything going wrong. Being too early may display proportions of your characteristics that may not be welcomed in a certain environment.

Jewel 122. It is not good to be a pack rat, but do not be quick to throw things away when you do not see an immediate need for it. This holds true for people too. Hold on to an enemy if they have something you may need. The term that I can best use is to recycle the things that have no need for at the time, to process them out. What else can these things that I have be used for? Then who else that I know can use them and if I ever need them back have access to. The people in our lives is the same way. It is very necessary to use people to the fullest and not have them in our lives wondering around trying to find their purpose. Even the enemy may have a place in our lives if it's only to keep us sharp. Like in a previous jewel, if we don't have an enemy that we know of it is safe to say that we must still assume there is one out there somewhere and act accordingly.

Jewel 123. A calculated risk is still a risk never-the-less. So, it must be weighed as a matter of worst-case scenario; What are the failures. Also, will the failure be so great that it cannot be withstood. However, a person who take small reckless risk without adding up the cost will eventually evolve into taking larger chances. In the end the type of person will risk it all. I smiled as I begin to type this jewel because who haven't been there at the place in life were, we decided after so many risks that it's time to risk it all. It almost always starts with calculated risk, what are you willing to risk losing if you don't win. This is counting the cost and smiling and saying I can live with that. In the process of failures, there are small wins that some are willing to accept if to them the wins are big enough for them to find peace with the failures. The only thing that I would like to leave with the readers in this jewel is that in any thing we do there are risk factors, even if we don't see or understand them.

Jewel 124. When a person comes to prison it's not enough for her to only prepare for a society that is going on currently. She must go beyond and make herself ready for a future that hasn't even manifested itself yet. It is most important for a person locked up that the world that they live in while in prison is ever changing. So, after several years of being incarcerated that world will take tremendous leaps and strides. When I was incarcerated, I begin to visualize what was necessary for me to be at least at the bottom of those that was trying to create value and rise to the top. I worked out of course, but I begin to take typing classes, and learning different languages. This world that I begin to visualize had not yet unfolded but I knew that individuals with a college degree of a bachelors would have a hard time moving upward. With a master's people may give you a five-minute window to hear why they should let you pass. Without that it may be hard to take you seriously, this is my opinion of course. Moving upward is challenging and takes the networking of about four wealthy mentors and leaders in your corner with an additional thousand linked to those that are in the corner.

Jewel 125. There is a thin between a genius and insanity. It is so thin that to look at it up closely will blur your vision. Whatever it is that is in the middle and we call normal is only a pigment of our imagination. People either hide the genius in them or the insanity. While most are afraid of the reaction that it may cause when they are expose, and the fear it may cause being different then people opt out and chose to live inferior lives. My most dominate thoughts are most often always what people will react to as different, weird, or out the ordinary. This is the genius in me, but until I can package it up and manufacture this thought in a way that will create additional genius within itself, it is best to keep quiet and maintain focus until the time comes to unleash.

Jewel 126. What use is it to know it's better to follow your first instinct, but never follow through with it? Only to hear yourself keep saying; I should have followed my first instinct. This is almost the definition of insanity, doing the exact same thing over and over and expect different results. You know or have the intuition to do something, where some say it's following your heart. Then at the end of the day going with a different decision and the result comes out to be the same, as expected. All you can say is I knew I should have done what I knew to do.

Jewel 127. Knowing the path is good, but to walk the path is much better. This is the great conundrum in our lives in trying to figure out our purpose, what is it that we want to do, and developing the means to preform it. Some once they learn what it is that they must do become frighten and run away from their purpose. We have all been there.

Jewel 128. Life is consisted of a great deal of things and some people will try to sum it up in one breath, yet it's not even about how many breaths one take but consist of every moment that is breath taking. This old saying is spoken in different forms, but it is true that the life that we engage in has these moments that makes life worth living. It is the natural cause of happiness, when one is living for the moment with no regrets.

Jewel 129. Some people, even though they have 20/20 vision; can't see the most trivial realness in life. These people were born blind and have never used their eyes before. The real and the truth are often looked away from and rarely seen. Life has funny beginnings and tragic endings, and in between the two is a blur and no one has a concrete story to tell of most of the time what is 50 to 60 years of living. People lives that are determined to contribute to society and our community will put the work in throughout their lives and never compromise with mediocrity. Seeing only the physical around us always get us in trouble. The old saying goes believe none of what you hear and only half of what you see. These blind at birth people only see what is taught to see, and no one has never opened the third eye to establish the most intrinsic parts of life that are only exposed through the eye of the all-knowing.

Jewel 130. You don't know what a good thing you have till things get bad, and more often don't know how bad things are till things get worst. In life we seldom have the opportunity to just always be in a good situation, and mostly forced to choose the lesser of two evils, is what we're accustomed to. This is more simply put the catch twenty-two of life. We are never in the mindset of the greatness that we are in until it's gone, and majority of the time when we figure out how to get there again that we are faced with so much adversity that we fail to ever get to that maxim again. Sadly, enough finding out the worth of a good memory is far better than the imagination of getting there. We spend so much time trying to get somewhere that is like paradise, such as heaven or somewhere with seven virgins. This is a misconception of what we will miss for what will achieve afterwards. Always remember you will have that one person that has been everywhere and done everything is that one person will say I had the seven virgins and they weren't all that and I've been to Heaven and shrug it off as yeah it was alright, not what I expected though.

Jewel 131. To suppress anger and rage that can easily be shown outwardly is show the strength of 10 men. Anyone can become anger and outraged and throw a fit, yet it takes great spirit and discipline to hide that same anger and mask it behind a smile or a chuckle when all you really want to do is reap someone to shreds.

Jewel 132. Poverty is the perfect flaw that will exploit weakness or the catalyst to demonstrate strength; even when this condition is overcome with richness, strength and weakness can be seen. So, poverty must be used as a tool for a constant reminder to motivate us of its lures and destructive devices, or the simplicity and happiness the lack of wealth brings. This one tool can be very dangerous to have and when used incorrectly can turn deadly. Poverty is no laughing matter and has the potential to raise up nations through the poverty experience of one woman. Some of the greatest men and women that have exceled to the heights of humanity came through the experience of poverty. Some after becoming successful may even speak of this experience during the opening of their presentation such as sleeping in the bed with seven siblings, roaches and rats. Covered with mosquitos because of the holes in the house. One successful young man that had a magical start often talks about himself eating out of garbage cans and being homeless. These memories are often looked upon to exploit their strength with memories of the struggle of being broken. Likewise, it is equally important to know that those that have allowed the poverty to weaken them will go on to commit crimes, make excuse for terrible judgment due to poverty such as drugs, robbery and prostitution.

Jewel 133. Drug addiction is an ongoing fight as any other addiction and must be attended to regularly with examination and re-examination; recovery is a constant process. My personal experience with addiction is alcohol and a slight run in with crack cocaine. The truth for me is when you first make the decision to use then at that time you are subjected to the fate of that addiction and all the negative results that comes along with it. Sometimes it is jail time, fail family relations, or even death. The only way to divert from such madness is the non-use of it. I used to have a problem with drinking yet found out through health problems that I had to scale back years ago, and after years of having to trade in sobriety for fun and foolishness, I exceled in life to the point that I couldn't go back to drinking the way I use to. My licenses would be put in jeopardy. Lose my family that trusted that I wouldn't fall victim of job loss or some disease attributed to alcohol abuse.

Jewel 134. When a people have been stripped of his nationality and his history, you'll see him never looking towards greatness. Then when he is mis-educated to believe he has never done anything great, but only to serve others, kills all hopes and dreams. This will make him accept that he is inferior. The history of the so-called black man, and Indians which are Moors and Natives are rich with history and culture and when these two groups have become aware of themselves will reestablish that greatness within themselves and rekindle the hopes and dreams of producing the contributions only, they can give to society.

Jewel 135. Revolution must be rushed and executed quickly, out of a moment noticed birth into existence and consumes everything it touches. When people get the whiff of an uprising then the preparation of defense can be hurried as little as hours, yet when it's done during a time of celebration and relaxation then all defense are down and there is no defense that can be established that will threaten the uprising. Many great revolutions such as Nat Turner and Demark Vasey was prepared for during the late night and unleashed while oppressors were sleep.

Jewel 136. Anything is possible if you put your mind to it. Even if you say that in 3 years you want to visit the white house and be awarded by the president. 1ˢᵗ you must learn of what type of prior success gets you there; then master whatever that is. This may seem complicated to the person that have no real intentions of even going to Washington D.C. He won't even attempt to wrap his mind around all the things that he will have to be challenged with. The biggest challenge is finding someone that have decided to accomplish an award by the president in half the time, this will leave a little cushion for error, and things that may catch you on the blind side. Doing the things that will allow presentation of a reward from a president will require a lot of work and a lot of help from everyone.

Jewel 137. One must become superior to their environment and find equilibrium among their peers; by doing this, all the obstacles that surround them will become steppingstone for achieving success. And peers will move more along beside you with formation. These are the true signs of a leader for those that can accomplish such a thing. The environment should never captivate an individual. In fact, one should be able to grasp the concept of unequal playing fields to his advantage and conquer his will. When people see your drive and determination then they will quickly follow suite and line up in a path that is successful.

Jewel 138. One act of love shown can ripple effect into multiple acts of love given in return. A sincere deed like this will not go unnoticed, and regardless of how it may look, love is blind, and it will boldly walk forward into the unknown not concerned with coming back. The visualization that I see for acts of love are always painful and even deadly. I imagine walking in fire for someone or leaving from a lighted comfortable place to go in a dark disgusting place all in the name of love. It is truly blind in the sense that the face value may not warrant the merits that will be brought forth and laid at its feet.

Jewel 139. A person that does not keep his word is liken unto a lunatic man that mumbles and speaks without understanding. Whatever he says is only gibberish and need not be paid any attention. A man of such means find himself not even believing himself and will catch himself after making a promise to someone asking himself why I said that, or how could I promise such a thing. What may have started for that individual from speaking out of his heart and then trying to fulfill what he said later has lost total value by the lack of commitment and determination that it takes in the effort to achieve sometimes the smallest thing, such as calling someone in the morning and wake them up. The lunatic man no one will hear and take seriously, and so should be for the liar who has said I'm not the liar I just couldn't perform what I said because such and such.

Jewel 140. One should not intrude into a person life if they don't really want to be there or have nothing to offer. Unless we have value to add to any relationship, or willing to leave that person better off than you found them; keep it moving. So many people are just wondering around and stopping at the first open ear that they can find and try to set up shop there if they can. A lot of times it can be for years, despite having found a listening ear to help calm what may comfort them and move on, it becomes habit to hang around. The only negative thing is that the individual brings nothing but empty conversation and nothing more.

Jewel 141. A small decision can be trivial and may not seem like it has a lasting effect. However, these choices that can easily go either way; later down the road can be so detrimental. It could change our lives forever. The detrimental part of life is the what if's after it's all said and done. It is often further gaged by the decisions that we make along the way that ultimately carries us to our destination in life. It is the most valuable resource to have different reference points to guide us in life through other experiences. Some people may quickly say, well that happened to them, things for us will be different. For an example Dr. Myles Munroe's pilot did not turn around in adverse weather when they had an event in the Bahamas.

It cost nine lives on that gloomy day. Moreover, Aaliyah the R&B singer, also decided against downsizing their load on a plane despite the pilot knowledge of its dangers. That decision also in the Bahamas cost 9 lives that day including herself.

Jewel 142. Sometimes the very people you are trying to save can be a deadly enemy; up until they are saved. Defending what believed to them is right with their lives. So, in order to better chances of survival in the process, one must systematically save with caution, while protecting themselves first. Even if you must back away afterward with a weapon still drawn on them. This reminds me of the drowning woman that one jumps in to save, and she pushes the lifeguard downward and fights him tooth and nail to bobble on the top of his head. This is what she believes in her mind to be the best method of survival. It is instinctual and can never be taught in the efforts of a calming voice, only to apologize knock her out and drag her to shore and after resuscitation hurry to get away before she calls the law.

Jewel 143. With age comes experience, experience brings forth wisdom. This common belief holds true only if a person acts on their experience and understand that what they have encounter in life now validates the results of what may happen when they move forward. A person that goes through an experience and gain nothing from it, then they have lost the value of why they went through whatever it is that they went through.

Jewel 144. When a man is locked up it could be next to impossible to get $100 sent in. Love is not a factor when financial stability is absent from the outside. The reality is a rinky dink job out in society makes for empty promises sent in a grade 1 job the answer to your prayers. My experience showed me time and time again that those who can will, and more often without asking and those that can't will hesitate before lying to you making you believe that your locker full of soups and turkey logs are more important than their light bill.

Jewel 145. Violence begets violence and cruelty begets cruelty, if someone lashes out in cruelty, then to respond with peace will greater chances of non-violence. If one was to master the art of peace, then they would deescalate cruelty by leaps and bounds.

This is the rule of thumb but not always the case when someone breathes out threating and slaughter. Yet with its proper mastery, it can confound them long enough to change the complete dynamic of the outcome. Martin Luther King Jr. tried this method and even though I felt like there were so many other options that could have been used, I do believe it changed the outcome more so than doing nothing. The interworking's of madness and insanity characterizes an emotion, so to deal with emotions and cultures of such must be navigated through precision and the rationalization of an insane and the madness counter-wise method. Just curious what would the civil rights movement been if Negros put crosses in their own yard to burn along with deadly traps such as pits and other flammable substances or everyone wore hoods and begin to attack from the inside, then the culture of our society might look a bit different.

Jewel 146. If a person must be inconsistent in moving, make sure she's moving forward twice as much as moving backwards. People always have the notion that time is forever and that they have all day all their lives to achieve certain feats in life. This Jewel is finding the art of consistency in whatever you do even if it is a bit unorthodox. Like the junkie desk method. Is it possible to figure out a way to do more right than you do wrong so that whatever you become your good will outweigh your bad?

Jewel 147. Each act we commit or don't commit good or bad, small or great, leads us to an unpredictable certainty of a conclusion. Does this make it predictable? Either a painful death or better quality of life. Whichever way it is looked at one thing is certain, this end will happen either 10 years from now, 10 days from now, or tomorrow. Each second in the new day we arrive to is filled already. A less complicated way of looking at this is not knowing what will certainly come. We decide in our lives to be healthy, treat people good, and trap ourselves around positive people only to some instances to get cancer and die painfully or some other horrific death by some violent act of another person. All we can hope for is the best chances of a positive end, and our decisions are the catalyst for this. This is where the saying stems from that life is not fair. The man that has hurt and killed many, may live out a rich pleasant life to a grand old age, getting away with crimes and damaging the growth of a positive society. This only illustrates the horrific truth that we have always spoken of from a different vantage point, life is not fair.

Jewel 148. We must understand that we may not be able to fulfill all our dreams because of unforeseen events sprung forth upon us and forces a compromise. Our dreams should be so vast in size that when we complete even a small portion of them in the end, we should be able to look back and still say, "I don't believe it, look how far I've come". My first thoughts of this Jewel are when I first set a goal to make a hundred thousand a year. From my studies, I've gathered that I must also set another goal to work as if my goal was to make four hundred thousand. This leaves little room for error or laziness. In the end, when the possibility presents itself that you may fall short, you'll be amazed how much you have earned. Those that set the bar high only to leave room for laziness and leisure will seldom achieve their goals. Dreams are accomplished with the determination that you can do it if you attack it with all you have. Not stumbled upon because you decided you wanted it. A many of motivational speakers such as one who was labeled eligible mentally retarded spoke of not achieving their dream because they set it too high and missed, but rather set it too low and obtained it.

Jewel 149. It is well for one to get a certain amount of work done, even in sleep as ideas and innovative methods in a vision are remembered when they awake. The mind when it awakes runs at 10,000 wave cycles per second. That is why it is so powerful to be able to listen to good speech, or if you were learning a different language in your sleep. This is a good algorithm to practice. It is a powerful practice to learn just as much sleep as if you were awake. When you sleep put in practice not only the proper sounds that will bring value to your life, but also have other efforts to have positive change while you are sleep.

Jewel 150. Never assume anything without reason, use an educated guess at the very least. This is the product of failing often and learning from those mistakes. Therefore, Napoleon Hill discussed the accurate thinking process, accurate thinking. This was from his book Success Habits, which expressed his principles in a radio broadcast in Paris, Missouri.

The Year 3024 Vista

Like John from the Holy Bible, I was on a
little island on the other side of time.

This is the sign I scene, even though blind and old
cripple and some said they think I'm crazy.

It was people everywhere, and it was over run
like rats, it made me lose my appetite.

My sight tricked my mind into seeing into this dim
light the humans that didn't value themselves.

Scarification, tattoos, became our new faces, Ball
room mask became obsolete not needed.

Death of course is no longer racist, dismantled beliefs
hung like wreathes with the blending of the species.

The old world never knew what we would do but, it
was left alive long enough to show you the coming.

The music recorded is blended with actual screams of people
dying and the videos have gruesome death scenes too.

And people just danced, drank and laughed as the beat blasted
in the background was humming sounds of the electric chair.

Nothing seemed right, because the 80's music all
sounded the same, just a little change here in there.

Then the 90's music took a lucky jump and
changed the entire fashion of how we think

Then when the 2000's came it became a
blended unorthodox mesh of holy hell

Sorry to be the barrier of bad news but the clues were
always there and some still say life isn't fair.

By Marvin Thomas

Jewel 151. It is curiosity that drives us along-side purpose; we question the unknown and become obsessed with finding the answer. This is what guides us to where ultimately our destiny awaits us. This is good news, and this gives us the strength to recreate you, and reinvent ourselves. We become curious about this unknown fact that will inspire us, and then we will make decisions according to the vision that will become less and less limited because we will gather the proper information and then we meet our purpose.

Jewel 152. It has been said," blood is thicker than water". Referring to family 1ˢᵗ. However, if the blood is of no use and it is the water, referring to non-family members, has become detrimental. The fundamental approach is joining yourself with those who have family values and principles even if it is not blood relation. The oldest tradition and culture known to man is the family system. It resonates with me the most that when we love someone and consider them family it is usually beyond the ties that binds us with blood. It usually is said through multiple events of ups and downs, emotions shared and other life moments that bind people that creates the closeness that people crave and trust that will be there when everyone else has abandoned them.

Jewel 153. Once life gets comfortable in prison, it may be no going back. We should see every moment as tolerable, but not enjoyable. Doable, but torturous. Life has made those that are locked in cages all the comforts of home. It in fact has made it more comfortable and those that are caught under the illusion most of the time subconsciously will find themselves doing things that will continue their lavish lifestyle of the incarcerated and famous.

Jewel 154. It is a lot of sick minds in prison who seldom get the mental health treatment necessary for recovery; except they are diagnosed, treated and given a fair shake; then they'll be left to their own devices returning to society worst off than they left. The true life story that I've seen in prison with my own eyes was that 99% of prisoners including myself was suffering from mental shock of being incarcerated. Some was more severe than others and most could recover from the shock with the right amount of family support, help from the agency as I sought after and received, and a spiritual deliverance. I would go to the psychiatrist once a month till she told me that I was straight. She told me boy get on from out of here an't nothing wrong with you. I had to make sure, wasn't trying to take chances and end back up in prison. The federal judge told me that if he was to see my face again that if I was to ever get out which was not likely then I would be well beyond able to draw social security. This was a wake-up call and I knew if I needed help with my actions that I would have to seek after it quickly. The Moorish Science Temple of America help navigate my thoughts properly, having two jobs, and working out was enough time to keep my mind occupied and bonded to the things that would matter the most in today's time. Ohh, I forgot I was also writing books on the side. This is the soaking of one's mind like a deer to clear the wildness out of it, and then that individual can run off to change the world.

Chapter Four

The Dream Challenge

Through social media sites like YouTube millions of subscribers years ago just started to heap freezing ice and water on themselves and others to fulfil what is known as the ice bucket challenge. Then they would call out friends or a family member and say now you do it. (crazy right and teens did it in this boisterous dare

Another YouTube prank that went viral and made its way all the way to the white house as moving camera's recorded Michelle Obama and Lebron James frozen motionless was the mannequin Challenge My 8th grade teacher Ms. Gainer, who saw something in me, she resembled my mother. She brought to light a glimpse of the mannequin challenge back in my middle school years. She had wanted to develop my big mouth that I had at the time to a positive voice in our school, so she encouraged me to participate in her Black History Month program. My part was to do a speech on Martin Luther King and a poem or rap of my choosing. The day of the program lights camera action (Blank Look) then the little boy drops the microphone and runs off. The principle comes out in the hallway what happened out their little fellow with stage fright. But you got to go back out there and face your fears, if you don't you will always keep running. (I can't go back out there right now, I just need a moment, wait wait wait out of breath) Then in seconds the crowd grows restless and the program goes on I'm lost in the oblivion of what could have been my greatest moment. Ms. Gainer comes out afterward and looks at me with discontent and tells me that she was disappointed in me and that she wished she had never encouraged what she thought was a great prodigy pretending to be a class clown but may have been a class clown pretending to be a great prodigy.

Her disappointment pushed me despite of my past failure to keep going. She knew that if she told me that she had disappointed me that I would stop at nothing to get what I want, to go after it, and never stop till I succeeded. I think this is the mysterious inspiration behind the Bird Box Challenge, inspired by the movie the bird box starring Sandra Bullock wearing a blind fold during most of the movie trying to survive. When you can accomplish goals and objectives with a blind fold It exemplifies mastery. YouTube has created all kinds of stunts with teens attempting to drive with a blind fold on which I don't understand because in the movie, they just had the windows of the car blacked out so they couldn't see the evil, and she used GPS. People don't won't to spray paint their car windows, so they drive down the street with a blind fold and eyes closed till they crash into something This reminds me of my favorite uncle James, who the family called Possum. He loved to play dead and as a kid I remember as I shake him because he wouldn't move or respond to me calling him, then he would open his eyes and scare me (blahhhh). He would get me every time. He was a short small man who had a hairstyle like Michael Jackson before he turned white. We called it a Jerry curl. One of his dreams I remember was he wanted to work in the pentagon. And as far-fetched as it sounded, He relocated to D.C from North Carolina and finally after some time became a Janitor there. I bet he told people he wasn't a custodian but a sanitation engineer.

It was a new disease that came out in the 80's that we didn't understand what it was or what it did, but what we did know was no one ever came back around after contracting it. It made him lose weight, it made his belly swell and it made him smell of infection, hid under the massive amounts of medicine that he took. One night after he had all his medicine and he laid curled up in his bed and he called me and looked me into the eyes and said Marvin, I don't won't to die. I realized what he really meant to say was he didn't finish fulfilling his dreams, his purposes, finish writing his life story. I believe his dying words was don't let him be forgotten. The next morning when I awoke, I slept to the top of the bunk bed my cousin Neil to the bottom and my uncle slept on the other side of the room. When I awoke, I let my legs dangle off the bed and stared at him. Something looked different about him this morning as he didn't move laying in a Fedele position. This time he wasn't playing possum. I didn't try to awake him, and I didn't call out to him, I didn't do anything but stare and as it seem time stopped for both of us, people came in not to notice my traumatic experience went on with the busyness of what they had already anticipated would happen sooner or later, my uncle who would teach me not to hang underneath grown folks, by pouring me a shot of liquor, and then laugh as I watch through my teary eyes, and hearing him say now go sit your grown tail down somewhere. He would also tell me boy you need to listen to your mother and stop being so hardheaded

My mother Gloria who I called Glo, A single parent reminds me of the fire challenge that was on YouTube had teens dousing themselves with flammable solution and then setting themselves on fire. Well my mother who was a single parent had a fire that was inside her to empower me and to raise me by herself to the best of her ability no matter what. Her working 3rd shift in a chicken factory encouraged me to dream, to push forward with effort and drive to get what you want out of life. I challenge you to refrain from being a mannequin take off your blinders and stop playing dead and let that fire in you burn uncontrollable until all your dreams come to reality. Dream Big, I dare you to dream, I double dare you

Life for me an't been no crystal stairs, it got tacks in it, boards torn up places, with no carpet on the floor bare. But all the times I's been climbing on reaching landings, turning corners and sometime going in the dark where there an't been no light, so don't you stop now. Don't you set down on those stairs cause you finds it kinds of hard. I's still going, I's still climbing.

This was a poem that was written by the prolific poet Langston Hugh's that was telling a story of a single mother that was inspiring her son to keep going no matter what, to keep believing, be up for the challenge, dare to dream. Martin Luther King Jr. also delivered this poem in one on his speeches, and these words have trickled down inspiring me, being the son of a single mother being encouraged as if it was my mother telling me that if I can't fly like an eagle, then I should run like a lion, but if I can run like a lion, then I should walk like a man, but if I can't walk like a man then I should crawl as if it was the holy ghost crawling upon me in a spiritual setting. I need you to fly fellow toastmasters, I dare you to dream, I double dare you.

Jewel 155. It can be determined if you are a criminal by heart, when you find yourself going through an unsecure door in a room that has been entrusted that you would not enter. Not evening knowing why you're rambling and searching for the unknown. It is little hope for one who think this way to duck recidivism. There is no rational for this way of thinking. I remember when I was a small boy, I wasn't entrusted to this area, because It was two stupid kids in an adult house that had no business there, and when I was left unattended started looking for whatever I could find of value which happened to be a gun. I wasn't looking for a gun so to speak, but it happened to be one under the bed. From that moment I started seeing opportunities like this more often but, thank God I was delivered because the amount of person that this equates to is a liar, a cheat, and a roach.

Jewel 156. It is selfishness to feel bitter towards family that has not done much for those incarcerated. For it was you that put yourself in this terrible position and can blame only you. It was only a few days that went by that I found myself trying to find someone to point the finger at after I was held under a million-dollar bond and it look like it was time for me to bunker down for the next few years. In times past I've had either my mom, dad, wife or a girlfriend to run to the rescue to handle all the legal procedures. This time depending on a girlfriend that I was trusting to handle my situation, and I felt like she was partially the blame because I was robbing people and giving her the money to repay her for a dog I lost, but that's another story. Long kiss made short, after she saw no way I could get out, I started getting her to send me money that I had left owed to me from different areas. She sent me a portion of my money and then after that took the rest of the money for her and her kids. It was for her the right thing to do. For me I was left in want and in betrayal. It was a good thing that it happened because it taught me early in the system not to depend on people outside as well as inside, even when it's your shit.

Jewel 157. Think not love is only an emotion, it is also a positive energy that cannot be created nor destroyed, and when it's sent abroad to serve its purpose, it will most certainly return to the sender more powerful. The iconic word we write about often which is love is hard to describe and hardly put into words. This mixed up feeling can be easily confused with lust as some say they can love two men at a time or cheat on their significant other and then come home and tell him how much she loves him. The horrific truth is that the powerful emotion of love it like energy, vibrations, and like spirit. It can be felt through a phone conversation, through eye contact, or just the way a person hugs and kisses you. Love is more felt than spoken of.

Jewel 158. Some people in prison are so detached from reality of life; that they'll begin harassing staff for a small entitlement so trivial, as days pass, they'll have forgotten what it was that they were willing to die for. All answers reveal themselves and what one has coming cannot be withheld if they know the appropriate measures and remedies to apply. Patience in this jewel will serve itself to the bone. I've seen guys asking for paperwork from counselors and C/O's that they don't need for months down the road, but the inmate has tricked his mind into believing that there is benefit to having the information early. Even down to requesting a book or a cross word puzzle while one is in segregation (SHU), that pushes inmates to violently turn themselves around and kick the door backwards as hard as they can for as long as they can to achieve only more lost privileges or more time in. Try getting a cross word puzzles after overflowing the toilet and throwing feces on the wall.

Jewel 159. Prepare, Prepare, Prepare, Plan A then Plan B then Plan C and then when you have learned thoroughly all the angles of every active party, and detail. Then search all the possible scenarios and pertinent possibilities, then you are ready to begin the road to success. Like packing bags and suitcases to go on a trip, so is life we must have a certain amount of already thought about bring along items so to speak. One could just catch a cab with loads of money in his pocket to a strange town and be ok for the moment but, it could be well said that the more he prepares for the trip, probably the less money he will spend.

Jewel 160. Contain not a wealth of information to oneself. Be skeptical that useful information may fall into the wrong hands to do harm. So, with caution take the risk to help those in need. Investigate them to avoid hurting yourself or others. I am in a marketing business that my job is to help people build their business and achieve a level of success that will take them to the next level. Yet I must do this at my discretion, because some people are not worth the time that you will have to spend with them, and I say this because they will only spitefully use you and then throw you to the wolves. Most people that are very humble of your help will show you by trying to return the favor way as often as they feel that you understand that they appreciate your help.

Jewel 161. It is silly and immature to not consider the impact of others when making life decision, such as pulling the plug on someone that is on life support or committing a crime. These two are the boldest of decisions, but it could be from not doing well in school to disobeying your parents and going off with a friend that your parents told you to stay away from. Every decision has a bunch of moving parts and the most vital is the result of that decision and all who it will affect. We just can't just walk inside a medical facility and find someone on life support and pull the plug, so is the same with all other decisions we make, who will be the innocent bystander of the result to that decision.

Jewel 162. Being in prison can sometimes feel like an experience of death, in visitation they come in to view the body then leave with tears. What those locked up must do is show signs of

life and re-assure loved ones a resurrection of a changed man upon release. I can only relate to this in the epiphany of the one and only visit I had in prison by a man name Gregory Van Black and his armor bearer Eddie Godley. These two brothers from my church made it their business to travel a very long ways to see me and for this I am forever beyond the grave grateful. When they came in to see me, it was almost like they were talking to a ghost of the past. In hopes that I would return, what would be my new identity and my new purpose. This is what we do when we see a body at a funeral home, we speak to the ghost and hope that when we see each other again that we be happy and at peace, after the resurrection.

Jewel 163. To truly know a person that's unpredictable is to relate to them with your own unpredictability's, when you can home in on their sequence and predict their cycle of action then you can accept them for what you know they'll do, or capable of doing then a journey on the same path can begin. It is like being married, but not quite the same. You both can't be the same person, so you will naturally do complete opposite actions. As you two grow together you will be able to not fully know why they think or rationalize the way they do, but you will be able to see it coming and know when it's coming. This is because you just understand not necessarily what they will do, but unorthodox measures will transpire.

Jewel 164. The good news for those who choose not to change or contribute to help others change in a positive way in prison culture have fully assimilated. The bad news is their eyes are unopened to the purpose of why their locked away from society and what good they could do inside and outside can never be realized. This is what society I think deep down inside wants people inside of prison to figure out, will they stay in or out? People make mistakes and a place must be designated for their actions, but prison is not meant for everyone. So, when a person has fully come to terms that he or she will be a full time criminal or a life-long rehabilitated person in the community trying to make amends for their mistake.

Jewel 165. A person can't win a lottery unless she plays a ticket. In the game of life, it is much the same way, she must position herself in line with the winning opportunities. Then with a

little luck, time or chance in the outcome she won't miss out. This is the simple law of cause and effects, if a person puts a lot of actions out in the atmosphere, then the effects will be most impactful from the response of the action. It is like putting a seed in the ground and having the hope that it comes up verses no seed in the ground with the same hopes that something will come from it.

Jewel 166. Everybody didn't come to prison to change; some elites of the world are counting on this erratic behavior to be able to gauge the balance of power. The world and how it turns was created to be able to have the haves and the have nots. Prison is big business and the easiest way to get money out of the government. During the time that I was looked up government allotted in the budget about $26,000 thousand a year. Bureau of Prison, Justice has stated closer to this time and era, as I went to prison in 2007, in 2019 currently it's reported that the average cost of incarceration for the Fiscal Year (FY) 2016 and 2017 the fee for the federal inmate was $34,704.12 ($94.82 per day) in FY 2016 and $36,299.25 ($99.45 per day in FY 2017. The average annual cost to confine an inmate in a Residential Re-entry Center $29,166.54 ($79.69 per day) for FY 2016 and $32, 309.80 ($88.52 per day) for FY 2017. For this big business, it is detrimental that people in high places control not only the money, but also the environment in which the money thrives. The laws that the elite proscribe is very necessary to facilitate the prison operation as well as the pharmaceutical world, but that is another story.

Jewel 167. Life is like poetry, full of vivid color, deep expressions, and wild rosy humor; then with a sudden burst of light it fades away into obscurity. One of my favorite Jewels is this Jewel right here right now. The most beautiful object among this world is life and the mystery of how it vanish so sudden is like scene in a movie that right at the climax of it, the tape has another scene recorded over it, and the life has only the credits to show what he or she has done prior.

My Records, My Remains

I awake in this glorious morning that's blessed to be
2015 where it's proclaimed that I'm free
My lovely wife is doing business downstairs, I'm upstairs
Writing this, listening to sounds on my T.V
Get my thoughts together then turn around and stare
At forever to see, as my aging ailing body
Is no longer present but still do you remember me
My contributions to man are more or less just what have I done
Once upon a time in Carolina I was locked up too.
In a concrete jungle, in this circus act of a zoo I was expected
To remain calm and see it through, was I affected
by the things I've seen and brought ghost back with me
We all have seen too much, when you take
a naked look into the misery
My mind is open to view the remains of what's done is done
The wind chimes sung a glorious song
when the dawn of morning come
For me to escape my time
And we say well let's put by genes all behind
And record our new lives outside prose by prose
Line by line.
Dedicated to Cerulean, Chloe, and Hakia

Jewel 168. Some people will do all they can to get into your good grace and fulfill you're every desire. This is only to execute their true motives of personal gain; It may take two weeks, months, or years but there are signs if you watch carefully and replay the tape of opportunity in their favor. Give people a chance but take every precaution to guard your endearments. Some people are excellent actors, but even actors take off from day to day. This is the hardest thing in life to want to believe and trust in someone, but they are only showing you what you want to see and some even say if it's too good to be true then most time it usually is. It must be determined of a true person nature of all the things that they don't know that they are being watched and judged. Only in the dark can one see a person true colors and then when brought to the light the person is who they are. A lot of people will masterfully trick a person for a long length of time, but the signs are always there, the attention must be placed upon the significance of actions and not the emotion of trusting a person will do the right thing.

Jewel 169. Do not hold on to a bitter grudge or lasting love that is trying to flee from you. It only hinders the progress of self-development in your life and disables you from moving on. Once you become stagnant and settled then life and personal growth becomes stunned. The truth of the matter is that we can't get settled into anything negative or positive with the comfort level that this is what it is because there is nothing constant but change. In addition, to be upset with someone for a long period of time will make you so bitter that you could make a lifelong mistake like manslaughter. I had an experience with a once upon a time friend who got on Facebook to call me out on some allegations of what he believed that I snitched on him. Embarrassment was to say the least, because you never want to call someone this especially if they are still in the criminal world, unless you are looking for some type of retaliation. I was furious and wanted to pay him back and more. After months and months of thinking how I could get away with an act that would show this man that I was no one to mess with. Then I had seen in a vision of all the people that would be affected by our poor judgement. My poor judgement for buying into his statement, he even told me not only I would know where to find him, but also what color vehicle he drove. He knew I would one day come, but this is the trap of all men who seek after vengeance and grow bitter towards a situation that could neither be resolved but easily walked away from. I realized to let sleepy dogs lie and only in the act of self-defense or protecting my family will I take a person life.

Love is so similar because when you are in a dying relationship and even though you are settled in and all you want to do is keep things normal especially for the kids, it could prove dangerous and produce pivotal psychological breaking points that may put both parties in harm's way. The only way to gauge, this accurately is known that you are in a relationship and you have burned the ships once you have arrived at the island of relation and there is no turning back.

Jewel 170. It is a known reason that people cannot communicate in a civil manner when one speaks in a harsh tone, they may get a harsh reply; so, seek to stay calm take a deep breath and respond accordingly, this gives the life of communication a chance to breath. We have all been in a situation where we were trying to win the who can yell the loudest contest in what started out as a form of communication. Then before the words turns into actions, character, and the whole bit, we must have a place where reason resides. This is where this jewel will have place to flourish and give domain to what could save an argument, a feeling, maybe even a life. A deep breath, and control the narrative by knowledge, intelligence and a voice of reason. Communication is a tool that if used skillful can control not only a narrative but the world.

Jewel 171. Young children have ingenious ideas and some of the most brilliant opinions, because they are innocent, pure, and their thoughts based on simplicity; For example, an engine repair may be questioned by a child is any gas in it. I have reason to believe that like what Jesus, spoke of in the bible except we come to the kingdom of heaven like a child we cannot be saved. Not impressing upon religion views, but this is a perfect example of the understanding that is required and to be rewarded must be in simple form. We as a people have forgot to think in simple terms to figure out what has been the answer in front of us all the while. Like cures of the past, and inventions, where innovated out of necessity and dire need.

Jewel 172. Eating healthy and exercise regularly can-do wonders for the mind; it will keep it fresh and rejuvenated. Just as exercise the brain with word puzzles and brain teasers is eating healthy knowledge daily; but what good is a good mind without a body. This is the portion of humanity that has the biggest problem progressing into an elite level. We only have halfway good ideas, when we are in our 50's and 60's, but our bodies can't carry us as far as we can go because of the late start of the idea with ailing body parts due to no exercise and poor eating habits.

Jewel 173. The truth only set you back so far then you begin to progress; while a lie sets you back perpetually to its gruesome end. Why do we lie? No one wants to hear the truth, and a lie has its fascinating punch line. When caught in a situation where the truth won't give you the benefit of a desired destination remember that the lie is only a fictitious vehicle and when inside it will pick you up and carry you only for so far and can have a blow out at any time. The truth is a solid ride which may hesitate to move forward once it pulls up, but after it gets going will not stop for one moment until it gets you to where you must go.

Jewel 174. If one can spark the mind of a thousand then two can cultivate the entire landscape of humanity. Another bible quotes states if one could chase a thousand, two could put ten thousand to flight. This may to you at present moment have no relevance, but it does. Tupac one who said that after all the millions of people he touched, his statement was that his purpose was to touch the life of one individual and that sparked mind would change the world. Today this prophecy is fulfilled in your eyes.

Jewel 175. Even charity must be distributed with reason and governed with wisdom. By chance you give too much away; it may also leave you in financial ill, or later lack the ability to act when most needed. If you give too little then you may miss the opportunity to fulfill the very purpose you've set out to accomplish; therefore, set rules, guidelines, and qualification in place so everyone is given to equally, and you'll be able to assess accu-

rate given ability. Most people that are in religious organization or have amassed a lot of wealth will have the blueprints of given. Most people just give out of their heart and not knowing what will be of the money that is given away. A man walks up and ask for a dollar and you give him a dollar, but you do not know what that dollar is used for, in fact it could be for the support of disassembling what you stand for politically, financially, socially or etc. But if you was to ask the man what is the dollar being used for, show me the vision after you have collected all the money that you need, and would a receipt be provided that I may claim the cause on taxes to continue to benefit the cause is very unlikely a man will produce if he just want a dollar for a beer.

Jewel 176. Do not allow sleep to be the only reward to your labors, nor a healthy wage to be a silencer to your complaining, but rather achieve in life that which is worthy enough to be read about in a book and tireless energy may be devoted to without earning a dime. This is called fulfilling your calling or purpose. It is namely the last day you'll ever work a job when you are doing exactly what you are good at, love to do and makes you complete. The reward of your labor is success in the fact that you found what you were put on the earth to do, even if you don't make a dime. We are put on the earth for more than to work a job, get off and drink a beer and watch television until we die. We must begin thinking individually how each of us can change the landscape of humanity, into a place that we perform the duties that we were created to do. Why is it that we only use a small portion of our brains, why are we still speaking only a few languages individually or lack the where with all to be great in our society and leaders on the planet. We are still plagued with racism and the dumbness of yesteryear which will not allow us to generate thought processes to carry us light years ahead of our generations. Most racist people say over my dead body, ill rather not contribute and die like this than assimilate into a whole that could actual use my thought process. The acts and deeds of our life will arise again, rather it be in a burst of a short breath the day after the funeral or in songs sung, presented in quotes and in books many years after you have passed form.

Jewel 177. It is best to take an extra few minutes or go the extra mile and be honest rather than lie; because in the end it could cause hours of complications and lies always has a long-lasting effect. This Jewel is very typical of the golden rule method but wanted to high light the lasting effects of the lie that last longer than the truth. The truth is enteral and undisputable, and people know that it forever exists but the effects of the lie, and so detrimental and cause the more damage and last so much longer, while we forget the importance of the truth. That is why we tell lies on the contrary instead of the truth because what seems like the truth at the time can easily be woven into something more and into what the truth could be. The truth is just so blatant and forces little imagination and brings us to the climax of the reality without any arousal of what could have been. So, what do they mean when it is said that truth is stranger than fiction? Another story for another day.

Jewel 178. When you're not going anywhere in life, step aside and let the next man through. It may be him that reaches back and uplift you. Don't drag nobody down with you. The crab in the bucket mentality has no room for those that wants to be successful. Each one teaches one and let us bear the burden for those that are trying to achieve if we don't have the means to get to the places that we are trying to go. It may be that if we are successful in properly getting people where they want to go, someone will ask if there is anything that you need let me know and this is when your hard work and efforts do not go unnoted.

Jewel 179. Rarely will you find a couple that has an equal love; for one will love stronger and more passionate than the other. Therefore, in order to better chance of longevity, it is better to marry some who loves you more than you love them. This is the epic adventure of love when you try to find the medium between love and war. It is more than expected to compromise and find every reason to succeed in a relationship with love. Yet the truth of the matter is that some people just love their partner more than they love you, so it's always going to be a compromise in this fashion. But if love is truer and stronger which is supposed to be then it won't have lasting effects or make the person feel like trash for over exposure of a feeling that is not fully recaptured.

Jewel 180. If you learn a foreign language it forces you to think before you speak, if you emulate a strange character, it forces you to research before you act. This is what you call a forcing system. Similar to burning bridges to not turn back or putting the alarm clock across the room and when you cut it off, then the T.V automatically cuts on with a work-out program that's screaming get your lazy butt up and get this money, while the T.V remote is covered with a picture of an overweight you. Toastmasters taught me to think before I speak because you always have someone critiquing your messages. Thinking before you speak is the pathway to happiness.

Jewel 181. There are two roads where a person meets and must decide which to travel, the one is right before you certain, but less desirable; while the other is far away, not certain, but more desirable. Every now and then you'll run up to one that's before your very eyes, not certain, and is desirable; but because of a certain situation makes it too far out the way and impossible to travel. While the first part of the jewel looks more like a 9 to 5 job, or a wife, life and education more mediocre and nothing fancy just something acquired because that is what everyone else is doing in comparison. While the other road looks more like an entrepreneur, with a higher level of education, with a model wife, with the attainment of having all the little gadgets, and toys of the world. The last part however is a bit more complicated. It is a part of your life that you get up, get dressed for a dream job, that don't nobody want you to have. You don't even have it. You with through faith and ambition are moving towards this path, but sometimes health issues, background noise, and other elements of life will push this vision of what it is you want further and further out of your view, with a bunch of sleep, snoring and depression of not able to have what it is that you desire.

Jewel 182. A man need not be to concern with his looks of being handsome, his true beauty is shown in his power, his charms shown in his wealth, and his sex appeal is in his bravery. The major question here is how we live inwardly and create an environment within ourselves that will create fulfillment and stop the comparison outside of ourselves. When certain subject matters come up about us, it will make us blinded about our outwardly appearance and more of the awareness of who we are truly. What is the true depth of a person and who are we really?

Jewel 183. Love makes the person smitten by it sees the other as the only object matter of importance. And if the one in love is not shown an ounce of cruelty by the other; then he'll be driven to madness and get them both killed. I have been into multiple debates about this one jewel, speaking about the story of emotions and what its ultimate effects on how it shapes us consciously or unconsciously. The action can be very devastating by a rash decision that may be prompt by the love of your life. It could be a decision of risking the lives of hundreds to save the one you love or having a state of mind that put you in a position that will blissfully allow you to say or do anything in the name of love. It could be looking into the eyes of a killer and without fear becoming a killer to protect the one you love. It could also be the acting out of emotion of bravery to become someone that the relationship isn't accustomed to. The debate often intensifies with a person saying that it could only mean a death from the mental standpoint that one gets lost in themselves, and no longer live for themselves but for the love of the relationship.

Jewel 184. We seek a small measure of peace, that few seldom find, let us discover in the greatest journey known to man, that inner peace found deep within ourselves. The story of humanity and the reality of life in general will be told from the viewpoint of humans, not animals, nor the plant kingdom or some outer galaxy essence in space. The peace we search for in this journey is to find the purpose of our being here, your destiny and, your vision of your contribution to the society that will one day be spoke of for centuries to come. So instead of the saying rest in peace on a tombstone, it will be live in peace while you are alive, in libraries, in businesses, in politics, sports, music, poetry, religion, and social settings, or whatever area that you dominated in. This is the only way you will find that inner peace and won't care if you died today, tomorrow or next year. No person should leave this earth not wanting to leave because they fill, they have not fulfilled their life. We should be ready to go knowing that our work is done and can say that it is finished.

Jewel 185. A true leader knows the ability of responsibility when they have made the right decision or wrong. The only difference is when he makes the wrong decision can over all still win in poor results. Even if he himself loses, it is impossible to be a true leader until you have failed. This reminds me of a high ranking officer who maybe have failed in saving the life of a fellow soldier, and this is what has driven him to be a prolific leader, and at the end had no second thoughts of sacrificing his life to save a fellow soldier that was only a few days old from being a maggot.

Jewel 186. It is impossible to know which the important days are until you experience each one's greatness. This goes from the first day of greatness when you see the vision of your success to the last day when you see it and say that it is complete, go on the deck of the yacht to lift your champagne glass with your family only to discover that all that you was able to accomplish was to bring family together hoping they will see the greatness of togetherness and be able to rest afterwards.

Jewel 187. Progression to elitism will not appear until several stumbling blocks are cast in its way. When this happens and each one is smashed to dust; then it can be seen, an elite mind that outweighs each circumstance and moves on to the other matters. The progression of the Golden Rule magazine, by Napoleon Hill is fulfilled in your eyes, but the many stumbling blocks from then to now have placed its many difficulties into a method that is proven to be successful. Elitism is a progression that sometimes takes many generations to accomplish through perseverance, and the renewing of minds and methods of what works and what may work. The elitist works obsessively with what they know works every single time. Most people stumbling blocks could be something as simple as a proper set of teeth or attire that will not attract the people that they are trying to influence. Either ground to powder the stereotypes that will not have you become the center piece as Edwin Barnes did to get his to in the door of Thomas Edison or live with the results that you lack the confidence to act on the big stage.

Jewel 188. Some believe they must aggressively approach their destiny in order to walk in it. I say that if you know that it exists, prepare for it and it will arrive on time looking for you. This is a portion of me being the bearer of bad news to those that want something so bad that they are willing to do anything to get it and for a lack of reasoning why they should thrive in that realm of what they visualize, people get stepped on, acts of cruelty are pervasive, and anyone and everyone becomes a victim of your uprising which is the beginning of the fate of downfall. The transformation of a person mind, what is already theirs to enjoy it must be properly prepared for. The good they will do with it, the gratefulness that will be shown towards those that helped you get prepared along the way etc.

Jewel 189. When you begin to enrich our character diversify it in the areas of culture, economics, politics, science, and spirituality. This is the tragedy of life, when you have a person that has a narrow sight in life in only one subject matter. Life is much grander if your perspective has at least four sides, a top to rise to and a bottom from which you came to build upon.

Jewel 190. Change is good but know it can be painful, self-realization isn't pretty, and at times can be overwhelming in the end you'll be like how did I get way over here; these are the baby steps that are so tremendous, when you don't consider the pain, you just go through with it. Writing these jewels that some will walk around with for the rest of their lives like a Bible, Koran, Meter Neter, or the Dead Sea Scrolls, is meant only to enhance their vision and where they will end up in life in turn where they will take humanity. The steps are simple, I am telling you that you will have the opportunity to say something, and so prepare yourself that when the entire world turns their head to see what you have to say put yourself in the best position to say the most important thing that has ever been put into their ear.

Jewel 191. Even after the world is tossed to our feet, greed still will not leave well enough alone. For it will want that which is tossed to be picked up and put in our hands. This is no more than having the attitude of greed, it is very dangerous and must be conquered before attaining a level of success properly. You can have wealth, riches, power, and position, but if you have greed then it is short lived, and most times met with a violent end.

Jewel 192. During the course of life, the people who you remember the least may have had the most impact. This is the distinguished approach of people and only reverences the powers to be at the moment. It could be the bum on the street that at first sight pushed you to never make the decisions that he or she made. It could have been the school teacher that said that you will never amount to anything, or the stranger that gripped your shoulder firmly looked into your eyes and said to continue to do what it is that you are doing, because they see greatness in you.

Jewel 193. Repetition is the master teacher of life, but it's only discovered after several visits. It is said that it takes 10,000 hours to master your craft, which is about roughly 5 years and some change. The repetition will bring out confidence in you because you have seen something so many times before, this is the master teacher at his greatest work. This is repetition bringing your attitude into perspective, and showing you that this thing that is being shown to you over and over again, while others have glanced at it and failed to see the beauty in it, not seeing the depth of it, the heights of it and every aspect and detail of it. Once repetition teaches you repeatedly every angle, concept, and detail then you can change the thing you see with creativity of a child into whatever you want with ease and without effort.

Jewel 194. A woman set on a mission has no idle time to complain about being alone, for what she has to keep her busy; is her company. Today my mother-in-law Janet Eaton, who has been alone for quite some time has shown me this jewel working frantically in the flesh. As I type this book, She and my wife are working together on creating a larger vision than their individual business, as they combine their businesses together and plan to open next week. Her company which has been with her all day, is not me or my wife, but her work of getting her crafts ready to be put into their store before grand opening.

Jewel 195. Always be ready to give the truth, at times however its best to tailor fit certain circumstances, for certain people. The perfect example, if an undercover agent has hurt innocent people along the way that wasn't directly involved in the case, the truth and the lie can horrible attempt to mix, but indirectly will cause unnecessary bitterness. It must be customized to the circumstance so all your good won't cause a bad situation. Preachers often do it when having to confront controversial subjects in the church and of course lawyers and politicians.

Jewel 196. Some will ask you a question that they already know the answer to with an interior motive. You should never answer too soon without thinking. You must have a quick response prepared for every question to give you chance to think motives at least. Only then can you proceed in a safe manner. This is the manipulative trick of people that starts with a question to gauge what they already know, but perhaps looking for a deeper honesty. With a slight hesitation, and with a generic response to someone you are suspicious of, like if you were to say I don't know let me see, tough question or hmmmm, while repeating the question. These are all response and gives you the split second to guess the motive and by telling them what they already know will give you the timing you need to not relinquish the information that they seek afterward that will leave you a victim.

Jewel 197. Death is the most common visitor; it often comes in silence at night and leaves out bumping furniture in the morning. This relentless visitor that always finds himself a guest at all our table, that we never recognize their presence. Sometimes standing in the shadows of our living room while typing or watching T.V and only being caught out of the peripheral. One day we will be brave enough to go over in the dark shadows or speak at the table and say I know who you are who have you come to see, and hopefully it will be just a visit to be in the presence of immortality working through a physical body.

Jewel 198. It is impossible to have a quality life when you always make mistakes and act indecisive. The routine we have in life must be cut from the cloth of success; even if our actions become compulsive and obsessive habits, then you still succeed. The force of habit action breeds what it is that you do all the time without thinking about it, a sense of second nature. Another words if it becomes second nature to make money, and it is compulsive and obsessive, as long as it's legal is a positive. This is when people resort to stripping, porn and other acts that society frown upon, when the individual is only acting in the best interest of acquiring money. The success part of it is another story, because if a person is just in a habit of acquiring money then it's by any means, but if it's a certain level of business, practice, or even some hobby, to become obsessed with it, will only make them great.

Jewel 199. To look at a person as a math problem is difficult to figure out and complicated to predict, While the enlighten person look at people as a math equation. There is a particular formula in place and all need be done is calculate the sum. This is easier than a problem and all is left to figure out is the variables. The enlighten have the means of probing and profiling individuals to find predictability. Like a sports analysis done by a commentator knows all the stats, and variable. This is how trades are made, teams built, and championships won. Criminal are caught by special agents and detectives that are enlighten in the area of catching criminals. The variables are the origin of the person, and their background. The systematic psychological mind set, and all other traits that can be formulated into a simple answer.

Jewel 200. Be quick, alert, and always ready; even when you're sleep think on your feet. This is a jewel that will keep you inspired and willing to push forward towards a goal, always. The only way to be quick on your feet is to know the situation, your environment, and those that are around you and what they are capable of.

Jewel 201. Mascara, lipstick and other cosmetics are dishonest, and it leads one to misrepresent; true beauty which only can be discovered naked and untainted. The true nature of any scene whether it is a human scene, or nature it must be organic. The covers that hide the truth for whatever reason is full manipulation and denies the transparent scene of life. Sometimes listening to a lie can be a funny thing, with the joys of having a good time, but the reality of the situation is true beauty is blinding in its rawest form.

Jewel 202. A child even though may be wise beyond his or her years need not be in a rush to grow up; the child must develop as the body matures and the environment allows. It was a time when I was very young and as a skinny little boy, graduating from the street to jail I begin to pick up weight. I became taller and even grew more facial hair. I wanted to grow up fast because being a kid had so many limitations, and my mind wouldn't allow me to be held back. Being what I thought wise beyond my years was me being foolish. It sometimes is a cute thing to see a little child act grown until they start doing the foolish things that grown up do.

Jewel 203.You shouldn't be unaware of danger to be able to handle fear. Fear is to question the unknown. It's best to have acute knowledge of the dangers, then live life best you can without ever acknowledging them. All you can do is take precaution then live or die; fear should not be a determining factor. This is easier said than done, because there are certain things in life, perhaps we have never faced that will make us plain scared. Some believe that ignorance is bliss, while other dictate decisions by paranoia and call it being over cautions. The real fear in life should be having the fear that you will not live your life to the fullest by the fears that have been placed upon you by others. As we educate ourselves about certain dangers then we have the power to make smart decision, but if we die then the choice was made with the best information that you had at the time, but the world stage should not be timidly approach with paralysis.

Jewel 204. Restrain from showing to much emotion, and never let anyone know exactly what you're thinking always leave a little wiggle room until you find out what's on their mind first. The important part about this jewel is you knowing what the other person is thinking. My ex-wife which was Italian told me to never let anyone know what I was really thinking. This was made mention because, the thick skin of individuals will more than likely find the result or answer that they are looking for if they only remain calm. People say a lot of stuff to get underneath your skin, only to find out what it is that you are really thinking. Yet at the same time if you shut down and begin to study them then you will know exactly what they are up to.

Obsessed with the Process

What are we doing here? Wait wait, don't answer that, because the question should not be what are we doing her. The question should be what are we becoming here. Whatever it is that we will become no matter how great, or insignificant it takes a certain level of dedication and determination. For some of the people that came on this day it was very easy because the decision had already been wrestled with years ago to become better and to do better, why other are deciding what is it that they are trying to do with their lives and perhaps waiting on a message from God to press send. No one just happened to stumble upon greatness unless you have the rich uncle that dies and leaves you his estate, Event then you must have sense enough to use it. No one stumble upon greatness unless you walk in the wrong classroom and accidently become a guest at toastmasters, having someone like Lynne Claiborne to become your mentor.

To become that person that you envision yourself being will take more than blood sweat and tears, it's going to take a mind set to drive that force. This energy force will push you past the blood, sweat and tears, therefore, the blood, sweat and tears become a bi product of the force. What is the force, the force is what I will like to introduce to you as obsession? For the sake of category and title I will refer to it as dark obsession and I'll explain why I included the word dark into it throughout. We will never become unless we first have an obsession to do so and then it must have a dark tint to it that it may fully develop like film. Who we are is never fully manifested in the light, but truly who and what we are is discovered in the darkest hour and then that image is manifested in the light?

Millions of years of evolutions has taken place in the womb of a woman to create a full body of a human in 9 months. This process is called being pregnant, and it is then that the obsession to live, to fight, to win took control of your unseen mind controlling thoughts. These thoughts, this being with energy that is now identified to be you fought from over 40 million to 1.2 billion brothers and sisters to get to this place called earth. This is not a sprint folks, this is a marathon and we got to the egg and thought it was the finish line. The process of growth and development is bigger than your mind becoming attached to a body and then moving through this planet called earth. It's the process of an idea traveling across an extensive timeline, a torch being passed from sperm cell to egg to embryo to sperm cell to egg to embryo. A message passed in our DNA that is also equipping us with the survival of the fittest body and mind set to gather all what we can and pass what we have collected on to the next generation. My last question is when we have finish becoming what will we look like? Can you imagine I use to have a tail and could swim? But, because I'm still developing, I'm afraid of water, how so when my entire nature should be amphibious. The process is where we lose folks because during what we think is growth and development can easily become misconstrued with being torn down and broken into a thousand pieces. The process is usually a ridged road that is painful, outside of our comfort zone and a many of allures and enticement to look the other way and let somebody else deal with this carry the great message from one generation to the next and one century to the next. The process can be difficult but it's the reward that gives us the inspiration to continue the journey. To become highly skilled, and perfect your craft it takes 10,000 hours is what Malcolm Gladwell said. The grueling process is what we first fall in love with, it is the pain, that was meant to crush us, we become pain freaks and become addicted to the pain. We cut out all the things that feel good and become angry with the things that try to take us away from what we will become. No matter if it's getting up early, staying up late, sacrificing at any time what we are at the moment for what we will become. The process will get us there, the process will further the cause, the torch of a sparked idea, the message that some are looking for God to press send on. It is in our darkest moment that we find out who we are, in the womb, in the negative that will develop like a picture. So, I'm not going to ask you what you are doing here, but I will ask you what are you becoming here.

Jewel 205. Some people are born into your life, some work their way in, and some are thrust upon you. This is a prolific saying I think that most people can look to the person next to them and see one of these three. Family members are usually the ones born in as the rule of thumb, but adoption agencies have changed the dynamics of birthrights and who is a brother or sister. The other thing is the lovers we have over our life period. Some fought desperately to be the only one to hurt you, instead of making sure that you never experienced another painful relationship. Then there are relationships built where suddenly you realize that you are best friends with someone that got drunk at the club and hopped into the car with someone, they bump into at the club that came with you. You look back in the back seat an there lies a drunk future friend that you had no idea was back there. Years later you look back and laugh about how you met. The people that fall into our lives everyday are there to influence us somehow. Rather born like family or a lover that manipulates his way in to win your heart or someone that ends up in your back seat after a wild night of drinking with friends needing a ride home, they are in your life for some purpose.

Jewel 206. We are the message we bring. We always hear about being the change that we want to see, and this works similar because it isn't what we hear it what we see to believe. It so even or character which should be at the end of or expiration date should have a story behind it, it is in essence a message.

Jewel 207. To have the job of reaching people from a platform is a great honor; yet those behind a podium can get puffed up, and only care how they are perceived by others; rather than the job at hand. Vanity is the only entity that demands such attention,

and when given into it, you do a great injustice to yourself. This is a place that people go sometimes and hide behind, and that is the podium. Then after hidden for so long then they are able to build this person that they wish they were, and it becomes all about this fictitious person that they hope will continue to hide their true selves forever.

Jewel 208. Do not aspire to skip degrees of knowledge. When you first begin walking, you'll get tempted to start running without having learned all the steps. Master one degree at a time and soon you'll be flying. This is the one fact of life that is the most important concerning knowledge. The light bulb when first designed had to go through certain levels and not one step could be skipped to make the light bulb light up, not even a thousand times. Airplanes, cars and boats would be something that you wanted every bolt and screw assembled in. The same goes for having knowledge of a subject and trying to deliver it to one source to the other. Without all the information you could crash, hurt someone else or just plain end up looking silly.

Jewel 209. They say all good things come to those who wait. I say why wait when you can research where to find the good at, and at least meet it halfway. More times than acknowledge we know the answers and know exactly where to find the very thing that we are waiting on. The truth of the matter is we are waiting at times because we are undecided what the thing that we are about to possess is going to be in good hands. The church has even begun to preach stop waiting on your blessing and stop praying for what is already yours. Go after it.

Jewel 210. Pain is good; to experience pain is to later be able to appreciate the lack there of, and pain also give you opportunity to understand what is real. The point of going to prison is to be painful, but it has come to the point that somehow, the system has made the pain endurable or even in some cases made the pain completely go away. Therefore, so many people recidivate, because now not only has the path become glorious, but I've personally heard people call this horrific experience vacation. Where inmates lay in bed all day only to get up to eat and then when they feel like getting up, activities are set for boredom until it's time to be released.

Jewel 211. Do not offer to help someone if you don't have the tools or resources to, you may end up wasting their time or leaving them worst off than before you found them. This goes beyond helping the bum on the corner, it can be telling a friend that you will help them through a financial difficulty. This situation can snowball out of control when your help is offered and they begin to consume their resources thinking that they have you to fall back on, and then when you don't have it completely in your power to help then they are in a mess for real.

Jewel 212. Fear not to search deep within yourself of what you might find. It may turn out to be something hideous, hiding within you could be a complete monster, but what is more frighten is not know the boundary in which it lurks. It has been said that in every man is the devil, and this powerful as I've investigated myself found that we have this dark side only to unleash in a moment of desperation when our family and loved ones are threated. When not understood the purpose of this hidden danger, it could pop out at a time that is underserving and unnecessary, also it could cause repairable situations unsalvageable.

Jewel 213. An idea is conceived and after it is cultivated spring forth into a theory out from it come a philosophy for after the age of time has rained on this philosophy for so long then it's foundation will sprout out a belief system. This is what we live in society a belief system that has sprung from some cultivated idea and be philosophized over time and in present day is fact. What I have found out to be true is that in politics, religion, love, or finances it's the same. The idea sprung forth of love for an example and that it may be influenced by religion to death do us part, political systems make laws saying that cause of different religions you can have one wife or two, even in the United States of America. Also, the saying has be spoke no finance no romance, so this structure of a relationship has birth out and sprung forth the idea that you need to have money for more love.

Jewel 214. Stay 50 moves ahead of those that if had the advantage over you would destroy you. This must be the most difficult situation to put yourself in because how do you know how to move ahead of those would use or despiteful use you. One move is hard enough, but once you figure out the first move of what they could do to sabotage you, then the pathway becomes clear to what it is that you will do from there. For an example, for those that I know would destroy me given the chance, I will always plan scenarios of what our meeting will be like and never leave destiny to chance or emotions to control the environment. This is reckless living and irresponsible on behalf of putting you or your family in jeopardy.

Red Sea

When her legs spread it was like the parting of the Red Sea
My eyez where amazed as if I was seeing the glory of the Lord
I kicked off my sandals because I was approaching holy ground
Gazing at those two round mounds, and
the nipples of mountain tops
Florescent whitecaps stood attention waiting for my command
I bowed down in the soothing sand and
inhaled deeply the burning bush
Feeling intense fire, and flames engulfing
me, lost in this tale of a wilderness
My hair turned Snow White, well at least
my mustache and beard did
Having knowledge of each other, leaving
nothing as Adam and Eve
Bear in mind this angelic softness was
inspired by a devilish ferociousness
As I climbed up to sea motionless eyes
red, in between to go through
So, I'm pushed in while I was staring there
from underneath on the shallow bed
Head up and in, on knees if we must
through waves vehemently beat
As the layers starts receding back and
unfolding room enough for me
Spread from as far as the east to the west, it
was like the parting of the Red Sea

By Marvin Thomas

Jewel 215. To be elite is to have multi-vision on the majority of issues in life, so when someone ask what do you think or how do you see it? While you're still processing the data from different perspective, you'll answer what you already know while gathering insight. This is the basis of being one of the elites and having those that are in your presence your complete undivided attention. Most will listen with a mouth ready to drop open as they begin to hear with amazement all the things you will say. With the perfection of how you tie in what you know relevant to the question, and even if you don't fully answer the question to their standard this is your answer and the rest left to their own imagination. Never say you don't know, and always give yourself a pause with a deep breath in explanation. Push to the limit with a question by either reframing the question to get more information so you can give them the answers or show them where to look inside for them.

216 Jewel. How do you complete a task that has no end in sight? The answer is by completing one step at a time. The trick is to not to look to far up the road. I wanted to write a book of poems of an example. I started a notebook when I was in my early 20's and just as I got my very thick notebook filled. I ran into some financial difficulties and all I remember is that I must slip inside a mobile home that I was renting in a trailer park. It was full of dishonest people so I should have been able to see this coming. I climbed through the window removed some of my items. A backpack with my poems in it and a few clothes. I chunked it out the window along with a few more items. As I left out the front door, I took all the things I could have replaced easily with a peanut butter and jelly sandwich. I forgot my backpack and when I went back in only a short time later, it was gone. I had a panic attack, a traumatic fit, and almost a nervous breakdown. My life work was in that bag all my poems, but I realized after I couldn't imagine rewriting all those poems over that I had the pomes on the inside. I kept the sayings in mind and continued. When I went to prison at 33. This is when I died of my old self and was raised up after 4 years and 4 months back into society. I started to write again I had quite a few poems that I believe would have changed more lives than I help destroyed. I was being relocated to the state custody to the feds and I had to mail all my belonging home, I mailed the poems to my grandmother's house. She kept them in a barn, and after I got transition months later, I got my grandmother to give the poems to my sister so she could mail them to me. Long story short, they eventually got lost like my last ones. I was devastated and wanted to lash out at my family because it was no way I could replace all that work. Then as before with no end in sight with Fear + Dreams x (Ambition) = Success. I picked up the pen with trembling and fear, and with excitement of now not worrying about completing the book but being able to keep up with it and not letting it out of my sight. I put the work in a personal work journal that are given to you in a psych evaluation. This is something that I knew would be accepted over the entire BOP, so whenever I had to go to seg, what some call the hole, my word I send back to the unit is make sure you pack up my notebooks. I saw these books as Jewels and worth more than money. Thank God that I was able to finally keep up with them and get a few of them published and now in the Library of Congress. I hope I live long enough to get this project into the books so to speak, I know it will help so many people and help people overcome so many obstacles that I had to overcome. It was no end in sight and I wanted to give up both times that I had to start over on these long journeys but when it's only one way for you to go in life, either gay, straight, rich, poor, ignorant, smart, weak or strong we are who we are. Embrace it and live with who we are. Elites in the front, excuse me I mean elephants in the room.

Jewel 217. Some say it's not what you know but who you know, I say it's not who you know it's who wants to know you. This is the quest in life to arrive somewhere that takes almost the genius, and effort of someone that is determined not to be stop. It has been reported by some that have made it and reported back that they got to where they were, where they were by the networking they had established. All about who you know right? Wrong, so wrong, this misinformation is only half of the secret success that some elitist would have you believe and not give you the grief of putting yourself in situations that people really want to get into your presence and pick your brain. With this thinking it is only a matter of time that you will stand in a class of your own and be sought after by so many that you will be overcome with obligations that will put you in a position in life that will be financially rewarding.

Jewel 218. You don't set out to change the world, the process is far too great, you must find what you love to do, this is when it's no more a job. You will act passionately and dedicated. Then only then over a period of time you will begin to change the world. Jobs are the accomplishment of others dreams. I understand that everyone is not able to dream big enough to provide enough income to supply their needs. Yet we will always have the energy to help fulfill the dreams of others as who work the cashier job are helping the passionate desires of Sam Walton to remain the largest retailer in the world. Ray Kroc is still franchising McDonalds and every day when we eat this unhealthy food at this very low price despite the damage it does to our body, we must continue with Rays agenda because we are still mesmerized with the idea that cheaper is worth more than the attempt of living longer naturally.

Jewel 219. Look at yourself through other people eyes and you can grasp a deeper sense of who you are; and if everyone sees you the same way, a clearer conception of yourself can be established. The eyes of others often reflect a deeper image of what is there while sometimes we only see what we want to see. The truth at times is ugly and hard to look directly at. The constructive criticism that we often need goes under atrophy. With a temperament attitude developed overtime will allow other to feel comfortable in revealing what they see in us, so we can see. Therefore, if your mom tells you that you're going to end up like your daddy because of the way you are acting if you don't change you will. People become successful and want to remember all the negative imagist that people seen in them and want to get on a pubic stage and rebuke them. The truth of the matter is what you may have displayed was what they had to go on, but even when we see something in a person, let us always remember to say if you don't change or if you continue down this path. We can never say a person will never amount to anything ever, even when people use these very same statements to change their lives and get on a public stage and rebuke the naysayer.

Jewel 220. Never get into the middle of a fight unless you are big enough. That means physically and mentally. When I was very young, I started getting into a little bit of trouble and a few fights here and there. I begin to gain a little weight and some confidence that I could handle myself. Yet I had got way ahead of myself during this fight that I was trying to break up, not even knowing why I felt like the referee, but I just jumped in. These two really wanted to fight and my presence didn't command the attention that I hoped it would in terms of backing back from each other because it would risk me getting upset. That is exactly what happened, and I ended up becoming a part of the fight as well with no real motive other than I got hit. This was a lesson to me that I should never put myself in this position unless I can make sure that I'm able to escape without harm or danger. People during this present time are often becoming victims in the same situation trying to break up disputes. Gunned down or stabbed to death becomes the fate of those that are innocent, and the aggressor are usually the ones who learn the lesson.

Jewel 221. The universe is always trying to leave us hints and clues. We often connect the dots in hindsight as everything else we see is in the past. Our image cast a mirror takes time to reflect with the light in our eyes then quickly process the information of what we see to our brain. We must not only see as objects appear, we must see clues and hints to be able to see in predictions. This is Universe foresight. The promise that we can be assured of in the future is that the past is a relevant fact and that is how we discover that which is before us. As vision has its way of showing us the refection through light rays and membrane cells how to collect that data to move forward. So, is it in the stages of the things that are before us that we must detect and learn from it?

Jewel 222. Everyone is a manipulator to some degree, even a baby without being taught knows how to manipulate. Crying right foolishly to get what they want. Some adults figure out the power and home in on the skills, to get what they want. Like with all power that can be used for good or evil, either learn if you are a person that want to get people to do good or bad or a person that will look to defraud. My psychologist told me when I was in prison that she was a physiologist lastly, but a manipulator first. I needed specifics and had no clue to what she was talking about. She went on to explain that the degree was to home in her skills of a manipulator and this generality was said that she was this all along. The kicker what she told me is that we all are, and she went on to explain. All around us in the prison where people that had gotten good at manipulating people, starting from early childhood. When people get good, they sometimes use this power for evil instead of good. Children often use crying and temper tantrum as a method to get what it is that they are after. Women have excelled at manipulation in relationships, usually dictating the financial flow, and steady tempo of development of the relationship. Men only thrive in this when they can get better than women and becoming womanizers and abusers. The truth of the matter is that when we discover our being and who we are as manipulators, then we use it for good and sparingly if it is to get us out of a bad situation.

Jewel 223. The media presents an idea and then further along dictates how the masses feel; rather in security or outrage. The powers that be, believe that the masses don't know what they want or how they supposed to feel, so this public media, "regulated by these powers supplant these ideas and make the people believe they came up with these opinions on their own. The news has a way of making us mad or brings us to peace with the realities that are brought forth through each media site. It is through each perspective of the announcer to what it is that the narration should be. Some elements may be covered up to be able to bridge breaking news from day to day. Some news just isn't worth talking about and some news that isn't worth talking about is all there is, and it makes for a cute story. I saw on the news a few nights ago where a young man stole an American flag off a fire station building. The news media covered the story where they made the young man do community service such as give out flags to people in the community for free. I remember when I was running around stealing, no one would ever give me the chance to repay my debt by passing out what I stole, or anything that would show a lesson of immaturity.

Jewel 224. Children feel pain and scream out holding where it hurt. While the adult look at the pain in silence and access the method of recovery. This is where men and women take responsibility and understand that pointing at the problem in pain want help. It is easier to point and identify than look with rapid speed to find solutions to fix the problem.

Jewel 225. There is no lack of opportunity, there is only a scarcity of imagination. This one thing that people have when moments come when we doubt ourselves. It is a strong imagination, a rich vision. We can't see fully all what we must do, but if we write it down and go over it every day then after we have put our time in then we will be able to see it as if it was in front of us written down. How many of us have ever tried to adjust a necktie in the dark bathroom with a candle lit because the lights are not on, and the repo has come taken the car away so you have to catch a ride with a girlfriend with no license but is riding around like she had one. Grass grown up high enough to hide people that jump out of cabs because they can't pay, or traveling on back roads because the bicycle that you still can't say where it came from, chain keeps coming off and you need to be able not have it come off In traffic. The way you keep going towards your dreams is having vision and imagination.

Jewel 226. The intangible power of thought is our riches that need not be stored. Thought is a powerful and rich commodity. In fact, with its enhancement of muscle memory, and exposed to the wealthiest aspects of thought which makes men successful. In the morning or thoughts operate at 10.5 wave cycles per second, which is to confirm that the best to enrich your thoughts are in the morning when you awake.

Jewel 227. The strong take from the weak and the elite take from the strong. There is always something worst out there when you think you've seen it all. Most people hit a certain status in life and then taper off with a mediocre stride, which is safe and more secure. It takes risk to get to the highest places in life and this is where the elite thrive and live at. There are millions of millionaires and have no fear of anything that is beneath them. Yet the Billionaire feed upon them as lunch meat and have so many of them in constant fear of endangering their wellbeing and financial health by buying them up into obscurity, it's like the hawk and the fish. There is a final question that remain, and it is who feeds on the Elite, are we at the top of the food chain, or just in our imagination. Do the Elite feed upon the Elite as well or is there a higher entity?

Jewel 228. There is but one thing that happens in an instant, and that is destruction…build something and when an earthquake come its gone. Everything else takes time; building a family, raising children, having a career. All of this takes time. Destruction is the number one way to vanquish hopes, dreams, and ambition. With so much effort and energy piled upon an endeavor rather it be a physical building or a relationship, a simple act of and earthquake or an accident that results in a death, can end it all in one moment.

Jewel 229. We must work fiercely to achieve our goals and objectives. Yet we must be patient as results come trickling in; till we can get them to pour. Don't be discourage because of the struggle, it supposed to be hard, we must be empowered by anticipating the end results. There is not a moment to waste once we discover what our life purpose is. The time it takes to accomplish just one aspect of your dreams may take a lifetime, with all efforts directed towards this purpose. There are always obstacles that are put in our path and the challenges are set in the way as stationary as the design of your personal goal or achievement. As the pouring of sand out of an hourglass, it is only a matter of time until the glass fills up. Tracy Brien a great motivational speaker and businessman often talk about the flash point after putting in so much work. Like anything that you do after so long you get better at, and then after learning from mistakes and networking through random avenues, then after enough time has been compacted all your efforts will come back upon you in a massive amount.

Jewel 230. Freedom is like air; you only notice it when it gone. Freedom was taking from me after I was imprisoned for 4years 10month. The freedom was seen from my perspective before then as a life that was necessary to play out in doing whatever it was that I wanted. I was focused on living in America and not the fact that some have never known freedom and for those that hadn't if given just a small chance that I squandered through the years.

Jewel 231. In the end the person who you will be closest to, will be the one you have had the closest connection to being understood. In life it's not totally about how much you understand a person that will be close to you it is the person that understands you. My cousin Detrick, Ty and my brother from another mother Rueben, understood me and that is why I push forward with them as of today. I knew all I needed to know about them when I knew that they could put up with my crazy ways.

Jewel 232. When you give in to fear you give power to it, and over you. When you have no fear then you give into dangers and risk. Rather seek to know the depths of fear and then channel the energy and use it to your advantage. You can get so much further in life without having fear, but it has to be a safe, and healthy amount of caution to the risk that we take and the more educated about these factors we are the better we can become at getting these goals accomplished.

Jewel 233. When a child loses their mother, they can feel their mortality, when a mother loses a child, they lose feelings and the mother also loses her immortality. This is simply the close connection of parents to their children. The child we feel a part of them laying to rest knowing that when mom is gone that apart of us is lying there with us. This is the cord that was cut from which we came. On the other hand, when a child is lost that thing that you are sending off into the world to stretch and push on your dreams and ambitions is cut short and all that dies with you now.

Jewel 234. The body is a miraculous creation, as it breaks down and then build itself back up. This is called aging, then one day without any apparent reason decides to rejoin the natural form of its makeup and release your essence or energy. Ashes to ashes and dust to dust. Life is so fragile and yet it can sustain so much damage, from a simple fall and bump to the head can kill a person while some can shoot themselves point blank range and survive the shot and live a life almost as normal as anybody else lives. The sun and wind beat vehemently upon our flesh day and night urging our bodies to age and deteriorate. Our bodies are not meant to stay upon the face of the earth for always in the walking motion, and forces some of its forms to flow as the dust of the earth or unravel at the bottom of the sea, until the time come when the minerals are many enough to birth out an individual.

The Ghost in the Mirror

The reason why will become so large, and the vision will become so extreme, that people will not have to see the dream, all they must do is see you. They will know by your actions that you have seen something that you have been touched by something. Your movements are with purpose, discipline and destiny. We should pursue our goals in a way that the bystanders in life need to pull you aside saying excuse me sir, please I have a question to ask you. And after you say ok what is it, and they will go on to ask you have you seen a ghost. With a smile and then followed by a serious look reply with the answer yes. And when they look on in amazement waiting for an explanation or response, you shall go on to tell them that the ghost was you, and knowing that one day you shall be no more that, this is the reason why you must do all you can do while you have the ability to do all that you hope and dream. It may be times that you will doubt yourself and feel like hardship has got the best of you. The repo man didn't see your vision that is why he proceeded to take away the car, giving you a chance to get everything out of the glove box and the trunk. The Judge didn't see your vision, so he gave you enough time on a sentence for two people to split up and come home and do right. The job didn't see your vision, so they gave up on you and fired you. Your wife didn't see your vision, so she walked out, and is the same for family, friends, and co-workers. Everyone isn't going to see your vision, and they do not see the look deep in your eyes that makes you unstoppable. The Ghost in the mirror sees beneath the flesh and the cloths and remember the young man that was hopping around at an Amway conference in Greensboro N.C over 15 years ago from this date. Jumping up in excitement screaming you want to be a millionaire. Many mentors have been this way to plant seeds and then move on down the path of life. In the mirror with broken glasses and adjusting a salvation army necktie with no lights on. Just the flickering of a candle burning and burning fire inside yourself, that even if no one sees it for me, I see it for myself. I will push on and achieve my dreams. I'll write books, I'll create businesses, I'll obtain a high level of education, and then travel over the country to speak to business leaders to help them improve their quality of service. When you can walk in the darkness and know your way around. Walking in confidence because you've been in this dark room many times and know exactly where everything is. When the light comes on what will the world find you up to. We got to zero in on our craft, perfect our trade, and sharpen or gift in a way that even if we are blind that we still can perform the task as if we could see. When we see deeper in ourselves, we see the one, the unstoppable, the individual in the mirror that has seen something greater and bigger than ourselves now. People normally can see only what is in front of them at the time, yet when you look in the mirror and see this force and reckoning staring back and saying without words, what are you looking at, go do what you must do. I lay comfortable on the floors of an abandon building with the mindset that I'm going to make it. Riding bicycles to work thinking I'm going to make it. Catching a one-way ride to a business summit knowing I'll probably have to walk back but my energy level was I'm going to make it. In the darkest moments we must be relentless, unstoppable, running towards our future as if behind us we seen a ghost.

Jewel 235. To accept diversity by those who have not yet been exposed, must be handed down in small measures. When all their fears and ignorance has been dealt with only then can the two co-exist. Prejudice is the wicked monster that kills and destroys for no reason. With little reason of the devastation that it causes and most of the time looks as innocent as a child in the face. This is the same monster that looked Emit Till in the eyes and began to bash him in the face beyond recognition because it was alleged that he spoke to a white woman. A bit over the edge but to add insult to injury that lead to death is that the two brothers who did it, and even admitted to it after being acquitted of all charges. We all have little difference in who and what we are. At the end of the day, in prison the murderer get along with the murderer, because now survival techniques kick in. The rich see only green, and the religious are bound together by their individual religion, so on and so forth. Then you have this ignorant mindset that only sees the outside of a person. This ill-fated mindset must die out because it was bread so rich and so impactful during its early stages of manifestation. We have no use for prejudice now, but for those that are willing to embrace holistic social living, beware and feed it to those who are without knowledge in small portions. Large amounts may choke them and scare anyone off that may already have doubts. Little children are innocent in the beginning and are without knowledge of the difference of skin color or diversity of background. It is taught through the parent's body language, their types of music they listen to, their personality of how they engage with others. The children mimic this at the first but through their own life lessons as they grow begin to take root and begins to take a life force of its own.

Jewel 236. To take away a man's son then he has nothing else to lose. This is naturally a man's legacy of his linage and without this, he has only the fact that if he was taken from him in a violent way that he may resort to violence, so on and so forth.

Jewel 237. The different perception from many people accounting an event, doesn't mean the information was not truth in their eyes. And truth is only one and need no support from another source. The different viewpoints only mean their interpretation was either fake or misleading even though they were sincere in believing what they saw. The truth is what is the truth, can it be seen, some people say something just doesn't looks right. Can it be touched some say something just doesn't feel right in my guts are telling me so and so. Does truth have an odor, some may say something smells fishy, or they believe they can smell a rat? The truth of the matter is all of those are mere evidence to lead us to the truth. It is said that it is confirmed these days through fingerprints and DNA. My best assumption about truth, that is undeniable is that if you look at it in the eyes, unlike the lie detector test that search for the truth in the beating of the heart which increases and speeds up. The feds are good at looking at your eyes and which way you turn and look and without saying anything you tell the entire story. There is a day coming that the truth will be able to be unfolded without words, we will be able to tell by simply what is not said and then by certain questions that are able to be asked with answer or no answer. The truth stands alone without any help, and when stripped through the process of elimination of little white blonde lies, what some call motives then their stands a young innocent naked truth that can do nothing but cry or get angry because it has been seen for what it is.

Jewel 238. It is better to be successful and look in need than to be in need and look successful. The irony in this jewel is no one will know that you need help unless they can see it, unless you tell them. I had one time became homeless and no one knew it. I still had a 1993 SC300 Lexus that I thought that when I came through a neighborhood that It was like I was one of the Gods descending upon them to give them hope. I still dressed well, and I acted a part that I couldn't keep up long without getting myself into trouble. I eventually did and lost everything that I was holding so near and dear to my heart. It was a relief afterwards because, then people realized that I needed help, and some helped, and some laughed and talked about me. These were both good for me, to get help and the fuel I needed to succeed beyond my wildest dreams, to prove them wrong. The fuel was also set to be able to return to help those that had at one point helped me.

Jewel 239. Friends with benefits is nothing personal, it's just the way the world is. Most people on a whole enjoy having sex with their friends. It's the added benefit without having the stress of a relationship that is set up like what a former world looked like ages ago. The tradition of marriage is still one of the oldest institutions known to man, with family values and transcends across creation, animals, mammal etc. The nature or a relationship is very taxing if certain expectation is the driving force of its success. It must be calm in nature, no jealousy, and a understanding that whatever is the commitment level, it the commitment level and if thing change emotional and a person starts discovering more about themselves that they didn't know at first then let the other person know. There is nothing greater than having sex with your best friend.

Jewel 240. Even though every person has good in them they also have a bad person in them. The art to master the two natures is to embrace the weaker and often challenge it with the stronger. And when the roll switches then the balance of power is a fact. It is the determining factor of everyone to their becoming who they listen to. That individual who is weak and ready to go with the most convenient way without struggle or sacrifice will allow the bad to be more prevalent in their lives. The discipled and the seeker of challenges will more than likely have a more level approach to life.

Jewel 241. If one hates to perform a duty among other duties that must be done. The one she hates is the one to do 1st. I hate to work out, but I know that for me to get the work that I feel destined to complete will be completed later in life. I must be healthy to perform these tasks if I'm fortunate enough to live. Get the worst out of the way and what is left should be a piece of cake. One last quote that you may have heard is do what we must, so that way we can do what we want.

Jewel 242. You can tell a lot about a person by what type of car they drive and what type of cigarette they smoke. Often in the two if a person smokes a cigarette that is cheaper than the competition brand, then the range of income is a factor, or if they have a habit of smoking anything when the cigarette is just a terrible smoke. It also is having a sense of pride with certain cigarettes like Marlboro and Newport's. People want to be associated with smoking the best and drinking the best. No matter how much pride these people have or economical insignificant they are when you see them smoking in a nice car, particularly a cigar, they may have a little bit of money.

Jewel 243. People you commit to and marry today may not be the same person you're married to 10 years from now. Love grows and develop just like the people it blinds. And as a person

grows and changes throughout the years may not be the same person you fell in love with. Before I get started no matter who you in up with down the road that changes drastically, this is no reason for divorce. Nor shall a person walk away from a commitment they have made in prior years because the person acts a bit different, this should be expected as the other individual may not be aware how different they have become. We must live, grow, and then prepare the exit strategy of our significant other. Love will blind us to a lot of the ill that is in a person and we just love them because of who they are and not entirely how they act. The bible says that love covers a multitude of sins.

Jewel 244. There is no amount of money that can save you from ignorance. When ignorance takes a hold of you it will snatch every cent you have away. Ignorance is incredible sound in substance and has a way of influences the masses. It steams anywhere from, style of baggy or skinny jeans, music that spreads foolishness, how we talk slang or broken English or even some of the violence that people participate in like the knockout games. Once people try to define foolishness and ignorance and display it for public consumption then it begins to spread rampant. The belief of having a certain amount of money that can cure the ills of ignorance will surely not help. Ignorance is at the equivalence of the bubonic plague.

Jewel 245. Some will not befriend you unless you manipulate and fancy them with lies. To tell them the truth will run them off. The average person loves living in the dream world, fascinated with fantasies and feel good stories. It is the naked truth that makes people look at themselves and their own situation. In moments of trying to figure out what it is that we want to surround ourselves with, it is not the truth that people want to surround themselves with daily that sometimes friends bring to the table. The most valuable friendship is when sometimes their opinion disgusts you, but it could be the truth and we should be happy that they had enough courage to not worry about the risk of losing friendship to deliver this assessment.

Jewel 246. Everyone has a plan until life happens. The matter of the fact is that you can't plan for life and that when it comes it is so unpredictable and that so many unforeseen things will come to blow our minds that all we can plan for is the unpredictable and the unforeseen. This would make for a sounder and more realistic plan. Life comes all at once in experiences and with blows that are relentless as the wave's crashes upon the rock at the shoreline. The only hope we have is to be able to foresee what may happen and then try to prepare for the worst of it, rather than assume all good is going to happen. It is like thinking it's going to throw rose petals out before us as we come through and sound the trumpet to announce our arrival that we are coming through so that all obstacles and hurdles may be removed until we pass.

Jewel 247. It is not a lack of time that gets us nowhere, it is having no sense of direction. There is only 24 hours of the day that shines upon us all. Yet there are people that will have more done by getting up 3 hours earlier than you would accomplish all day by time you would get up. We must act relentless and with a sense of desperation, when it comes to accomplishing our goals and objectives. The time has never been the factor as some will contemplate this in older age wondering why God or Life didn't give them more time. The truth of the matter is that we all probably have had way more time to address the issues that we wanted to conquer, but the sidetracked life styles we live will only reveal itself to us in old age in the rocking chair at home or the wheelchair at the rest home.

Jewel 248. If you have no idea where you are going in life then you will end up in no specific place, not that this place is good or bad, but to have arrived because of determination would have changed everything. This is one of the pursuits of happiness, wealth and tranquility. When we have determination to arrive at a certain place in life and we finally get there is an amazing thing. Tactfully as we arrive with whatever we had in mind to conjoin with our goals will make it all worth it. Some people don't have a clue where they are headed in life and that's ok for now, if when you do figure it out that you do not procrastinate and push those dreams and goals on the back burner. We must always be in a perpetual state of striving to go somewhere and in doing something.

Into the Deep Blue

Rahha Rahhha as you mimic the sound of the
Dinosaur ready to bite and terrorize

In the fiery eyes of your little soul you felt like
excruciating cries could get you what u want

I remember when you were so frightened of me,
I imagine you just didn't know who I was

Then you became excited one day to push your
favorite little truck to me, to push back

Was it because I'm a black guy, one of the few
up close you had come in contact with?

It's an urban legend and folk myth that people
looks can insinuate danger from black a color

The Yellow creed of your grandmother has
brought safety to culture through your Dad

The White Seed from your grandfather has taught
you if you get something you must want it bad.

Dinosaurs, toy cars and little soldier action
figures will like us all fade and pass away

What more else can I say to my grandson,
but to stay true, and do what you do

We are all counting on you to, till we
meet again into the deep blue

Dedicated to: Cerulean King-Sass

Jewel 249. We must vigorously act everyday of our lives as salesman, selling our ideas our dreams, our inspiration to those in power to convince them of our convictions. Even though our plan may revolutionize entire markets, if you are unable to convince them, your dream is of no effect. The real salesman of the world never become discourage of someone that doesn't buy their idea. The goal is to make sure that the consumer is educated and then, understands why he needs the help of the salesman to be able to graciously receive the product that will be given to the individual and able to benefit from it. The world has a dynamic math equation to success, and it has the highest probability of getting solved when, the persuasion of first getting a person to become motivated enough to do it.

Jewel 250. Literature does not die unless the culture of the creator becomes victimized by genocide and fall into the grave of silence, thus being erased from minds with bonfires. My absolute and perfect example is poetry. This dying work of art has not been upheld by society and the culture that came with it for some time in this day and age. Time has waged war on poetry because very few has stepped up to honor or pay homage to the culture that it brought. Many that are reminiscent of the genre that has seen the extermination of this profound art only speak of its existence in memory and have no courage to present a stand to stop the violence on poetry, self-help, certain music, artwork etc.

Jewel 251. Always try to stay ahead in life, if you ever let it get in front of you; it will drag you to your demise. Life simply put is what you make of it, but you got to stay ahead of the game. When you get behind the 8 ball it is a must that we know exactly what our next move is and where we are headed to next. In dealing with today's problems, it is difficult to assess the damage of what harm has been created until you are fully in position for sure submission. We must fight to the very end to stay ahead and when disaster strikes, we must be able to see it coming and not at least if we can dodge it or has it sealed our fate.

Jewel 252. Sometimes doing the right thing at the wrong time is just as wrong as doing the wrong thing at the wrong time. Wait for the right time and then do the best you can with right

intention. This may seem a bit trivial on one hand and on the other a bit condescending to say wait for the right time, because deep down we all want to do what is right, but the timing is never convenient. Then we turn to our own devices and use our best understanding in terms of doing what we can with what we got. Some say it's better to do something instead of nothing and then the quote it's better to ask for forgiveness rather than permission. It is the most obvious of this quote that we may not be able to do all that we want to do, which is the correct thing to do, but within all that is within us do what we know is right and make excuses, lie, cheat or steal to do that thing which is right. I used to lie and tell people that I was on probation, therefore I couldn't smoke weed, when I just didn't want to for my job that did random drug screening. I would also make excuses not to drive drunk and make other people drive instead of taking chances or cheat my way to success by saying that I have had great results from a product that I know is good, and will bring them the desired results they need but want you to endorse the product.

Jewel 253. A responsible person work is never done, they always have goals to accomplish and then later manage them. Its only 24 hours in a day and responsible people see this as a negative. It's the limitation that we start fighting against as soon as we come into emotional grasp of what that really means. The time we spend making money at the end of the day knowing that it has no real long-lasting merits in our society or the world, despite of we do it anyway. With the little time we have and know unless we use time compaction and compile all of our efforts into the one thing that means the most, we are as useless as the dollars that we work so tireless every day for in the wallet of a dead man. We must work diligent sometimes both day and night to take the responsibility of changing the world and doing our part. Lastly let me say that it is each one of our responsibility to make sure we leave the world a better place than it was when we came into it.

Jewel 254. There are more opportunities to commit crimes and go to prison, than education and going to college. The great paradox of life is that the world needs the bad things to happen just as well as the good. It helps balance out our society, create jobs, and gives people who don't have a lot of the bad happing to them to understand how lucky or blessed they are. Cops, Lawyers, Judges and Politicians need jobs in this field, and it pays good. To decrease crime is to spike employment. Not only that the rehabilitation system doesn't even specify if the mission of prison is punitive or rehabilitative. Work programs are increasing but most times are very scares, while drugs and other criminal opportunities run rampant in our communities.

Jewel 255. It should be second nature to do the right thing and complex and difficult to do that which is wrong, when we find ourselves without fear of the consequences. Those that go to church, moscs, kingdom hall, and other religious temples have a better understanding of why the fear of doing wrong is necessary. It has punishment aspects, what some call Karma, and other disciplinary actions when certain rules are broken. The truth of the matter is most rules are in place for a reason and if it's got to be a hell below for you to do the right thing then for some so be it. Others are motivated by money, good health or just don't mind doing what's right in the eyes or our creator.

Jewel 256. Keep in mind while in prison you are still doing time, as if you're out in society. While in prison it's best to keep at a quick pace of activity exercising growth and development. This is all with hopes that you will be able to stay competitive with the society upon release. Growth is stunned to those in prison that don't exercise their mind to a certain degree. Keeping up with current events can only take you but so far. It comes to a point that you must get ahead of what is going on out in society by taking classes and connecting with technology. It is in the best interest of the individual inside to also have a large part of him remain inside in order to keep sanity. Yet 1/3 of a person mental is plenty to thrive outside with imagination, virtual reality thoughts and self-development techniques that will keep them up to speed on the day of release.

Jewel 257. Never defect from a good idea, because it may be difficult at the time of conception to do anything. Only let the idea step aside that another idea more achievable can pave the way for the one less achievable. Most ideas when they come, it's not quite time for the arrival, like the birth of a baby. The conception is immediately and then it takes 9 months before the actual arrival. This is the same with an idea. It must be brought forth with pain, suffering and patience. So, with the idea in mind, let it simmer and launch ideas that are ready to come forth and support ideas previous came up with. Businesses can support other businesses and so on and so forth. Good ideas for the most part are never meant to be shoved to the back of our minds so far, only set aside where we can see them and see where they will fit when the next idea comes along.

Jewel 258. The truth will always be stranger than lies. This is the phenomena of sound bit, how it sounds. When we hear the truth sometimes it tingles our ears. Yet when times come that life is so graphic, words must be softening up a bit to be able to process. This is more than likely just a common lie. We are unfamiliar with the truth that is why we speak of it as sounding strange. The truth of the matter is sometimes when concerning a certain situation, tell me a lie until you know that I can handle the truth. Here is an example, when I first got locked up, I was told that I'll make bond shortly after and I would be back to life as usual. These was words of comfort at the time, then as time went on, with bond reductions and lawyers dropping charges that were meaningless. Then the final two charges left, which were gun charges where the ones that the Feds picked up. I was told a few more lies that if I was cooperative and shared my part in the obstruction to justice then I wouldn't do any time. The fact of the matter is that after all this time almost a year has gone by in hopes that I wouldn't do any time. It was only then I could handle the truth that my girlfriend at the time Melissa told me, that the feds was going to pick me up, I was going to do some time, and if I was still interested in her after that time, come find her, I'll know where she be—exact words. The truth hurts because we don't know it intimately yet.

Jewel 259. You must learn to look at yourself and love you, because if you don't who will, and if you do others will follow suit. This is a saying no truer, than life. Here is a way to look at it, when you have a business, that you refuse to invest in, you refuse to believe in or even use the same products that you sale to others, then It is almost a guarantee that no one else will want to buy these products from you. It is the same with loving and believing in yourself.

If you don't who else will, therefore you must do to yourself as you want others to do on to you.

Jewel 260. To sit down and discuss with a devil at a table how to go into battle is far better than to go into battle with a devil you have never met. This is assuming that there are rules of engagement, and there have been times were in war surrender and how to do it was a question. Rather it be sounding a bell or waving a white flag, so that all parties would understand the ramification of the war, Hostages are sometimes taken but often if they are wounded they are killed, but in the rules of warfare it could be in law, to take no hostages, these rules where established to make the men feel a little bit safer and to give hope even in lost, even when at times there was no hope. The devil will sit to the table and lie through their teeth at times in warfare, so when you discover the first sign of dishonesty in the devil all parties know what the remainder of the discourses would be. It can be lastly stated to always trust the devil to do what you know he will do and understand his capabilities, but if you don't know them then it's a bit harder to defend.

Jewel 261. If I know the truth and do not tell those who lack the truth, then I am worthy of it. And if it be a brother or sister, and they do not except it, then how can they be a brother or sister. It is often that we do not except the truth very well. It should be that certain things as elites that we should keep to ourselves. It's just a matter of having certain level of conscious and trying to wake everyone up with it. This to some cultures is looked at as disrespectful to try to enlighten those who will never do anything with the knowledge that you will give to them anyway. It can also be looked at in the business world with the 1%. It is a fact that people don't like casting their Jewels or pearls before the swine. It can be looked at from the point of the Circle Seven, when the prophet said that he could not awake everyone up at once because they might tear something up. The Holy Bible also says do not throw your pearls before the swine. This is magnified to the point that when you have something worthy of greatness you have to be careful what you do with it, and also those that hands it falls in may misuse whatever it is that they was not worthy of having in the first place.

Jewel 262. First, we must slow down and look before us, reflect on our own experience, then only then can we move ahead with purpose, power, and meaning. To know fully where we are headed in life, we must have a slow take off to make sure that we are making all the right moves. It is then necessary to access the situation and then pick up speed and then aptitude. The trajectory of where we end up must be discovered before we make our first move because everything could be at stake when we start accelerating speed. Our purpose will be discovered in our very own experience. No matter if you are in prison for 20 years you have a purpose, there is a meaning for your life. I found my meaning in prison and the people that impacted my life the most, where those in my life the closest, and it came full circle in prison. I learned who was there for me, who wasn't and what circles that I needed become a part of. Through all my experiences, I've learned who I am, what is my destiny, and what is the meaning of my life.

Jewel 263. Accepting the facts of our own individual lives, rather how unfair our circumstances are, it matures us into feelings of pleasure and happiness alongside grief. Having mixed feelings about what we think of life is perfectly normal, but I think that the most important thing to remember whatever it is that life has us going through and whatever the feeling may be. Make sure that those emotions run parallel with the opposite to some degree to level us out. Never be so happy to the point of exhaustion something bad may come around the corner and shock our world. Grief on the other hand has no place in life more than a few days at any given time, then it must perish.

Jewel 264. Do not let others be responsible for your joy, cause their harshness, happiness comes from within. This is when people let others build them up just so that they can rip them apart, like movie sets. It is very important to know that people can give us a good feeling with complements and flatter, which can easily turn into harsh criticism and backbiting. Within us we harness the power to make ourselves feel good about even the most trivial thing. Never give anyone that power to control that narrative for you. They are sure to misuse it.

Chapter Seven

12 Tools to Mastery of Self

An't nobody messing with you and you running around here eating out of trash cans, this is what Dee Dee said to Eric, many know of him as the Hip Hop Preacher. Dr. Eric Thomas but his beginnings where very humbling and he found his Why, He pulled it together and he got the girl. Through the eyes of a schoolteacher Mr. Washington he saw something in a knotty headed little boy, who responded to him when he asked him to work a problem out on the board, Well I can't sir I'm eligible mentally retarded. When this little boy school mates called him the dumb twin, grew up to sleep on office floors and taking a bath in the sink on the 21 floors to pursue his dreams, ended up becoming one of the most renowned motivational speakers in the world. He worked on self and his why was his mama Mrs. Mami Brown which his goal was to buy her a house. Sorry girls I already bought some girl scout cookies, which is the flat out lie Jim Rohn told to some little girl scouts, because he didn't have not a single dime to spare. His why was an internal battle to see himself in the reflection of the eyes of those little girls that knew he was lying, and he had to live with being lesser than a man of many means. This drove him with his why to develop himself into a person that would live with discipline, and principles. A self-developer must first discover a reason why he must become. Next is what will be the tools and resources that connect us to the fulfillment of our goals and objectives.

These Tools that I am going to put in your tool bag is for the workshop of the mind, and it is true a craft man is known by the type of tools he carries. I was birth into this self-development mindset when I first came home from prison being prepped to go back into what we called the world. I had all kinds of master teachers, and mentors that pushed me over the edge into where I am now. I rested then so that I could be wide awake now and build the perfect temple of man. My humble beginnings came about in the first chapter of my arrival home, I call the rose that grew through concrete. I started out as a labor in concrete and on my first day, when the concrete ran short of the pour, one of the older men said ahh run to the truck and get the concrete stretcher. I took off and when I got to the truck, I searched diligently looking for this tool. Only people who have worked concrete will understand what it is that I'm talking about. After a few minutes passed, I said man them dudes got me. Jokes on me! When I came back, they were laughing and laughing. The valuable lesson in this story is movement is not an indicator of progress, nor looking for tools and resources that don't exist. We should always have a clear vision of what it is we are looking for, why we are looking for it, where to look for it at, and how to use it when we find it. It always fascinated me to see the main guys that was running the job just stare at the Blueprints. Item number one is the most important and this is the blueprints, or some will call the plans. This moreover our goals and objectives as some will narrowly put it, because at the end of the day that's all it will be on some sheet of paper written down if you are somewhat attempting to accomplish them. It's always good to have something to remind you of what it is that you need to accomplish but just mere having the obtained goal at the end is not enough. I got some dream builders in here right now with a piece of paper in their pocket saying that they want to earn in excess of $100,000 dollars or more. How to do it is a much harder task so writing it down and saying daily devotions won't get it either. A detailed schematics out-lines drawn out in detail, with references that have committed at least 10,000 hours into the craft as your guide, only then are you somewhat on the right path. Then the reminders that you keep always lead you back to the blueprint that you will begin to remember and study and act out in early construction. Before construction can start on any job site, certain inspector is involved to make sure that things are done properly and correct. A rule of thumb, for you these inspectors you will come to know as mentors and coaches, who will guide you, make sure that you are not cheating a process early that could be vital to the latter parts of the structure. The initial layout is to outline every detail and calculate the steps of how many, which way will they take us so on and so forth. After this you put in the mirror, the little notes that remind us of our goals and objectives, that keep us focused and on time management. These blueprints after under careful review, will give us a visual image to grasp and not some fuzzy unclear object to pinch in the air at. Blueprints also gives us multiple phases that will bring the structure to reality. Different viewpoints and different analytics that allow us to give references to a constructed pattern and a timeline. The metrics will measure out, as blueprints has a key legend to be able to refer certain shorthand numbers, on a broader scale. Lastly, it is the most important part as you go through the pages of your plan, from different viewpoints that when laying the product out and having all the material ready, the rest of the tools will be pulled out to finish the final product. 1. Blueprints 2. Scale 3. Hammer 4. Nails 5. String line, or Chalk Line 6. Compass 7. Square 8. Transit Level 9. Hand Level, or Straight Edge 10. 12-inch stick ruler or, 33 feet tape measure 11. Knife 12. Red construction Pencil. These are the 12 tools to mastery of self, and with them will develop the mind which is a workshop into the perfect temple of man. The scale that will be used to measure your success directly from blueprint to real world development. It could be also looked at as other individuals that are doing what you want to do. Next money will be the measurement and how many lives you change or influence along the way. The hammer is the motivational strategy that will hammer home the message that will hold together all the content that you are constructing together. To push and drive the meaning of what is about to transpire through hard work, effort and passion. The nail is the knowledge, the data, the bold statements that are going to hold the product together. The string line and chalk line working one in the same will be able to pinpoint from A to B the straight line that needs to exist for you to achieve your goals and objectives. It is the truth that is reflected in a straight line and the chalk on it is to pop it and make that truth known and visible on that which already exist. The compass is one of the most important tools in self-development because it will be the tool to build a circle around you that will be very important to what the finish product look like. You show me your friends, and I'll show you your future is what Dan Pena says. The square is the wall that must fit at the 90-degree angle. It is where mentors guide you and manage movements that are also measured into what you will become. The transit level is being able to have clear sight from a distance, and measure what the height and depth is of man, his dreams, his ambitions. It could be done through workshops and conferences. The hand level does much of the same, but the measurements are up close and personal, at one on one meetings with leaders in your field or phone conversations. The straight edge will identify what is true and give reference to everything that is not. The 12-inch stick ruler is the measurement to the simple levels of what it takes to become productive, powerful, and successful in what it is that you need to accomplish. The 33 feet tape measure is the example of degrees that is required to understand about self, elites in the room. This is the very important to understand the mechanics of each degree and law. The knife is to sever the connection to any binding element that does not bring you closer to your goals and objectives. This includes deleting contacts, on your Facebook Instagram and twitter. Clean our phones and rolodex up so that all our relationships are coordinated and all others that come into our lives are invited in and are guest which should be treated as such. Lastly, the red construction pencil is very important to have ready and handy. It will check off different elements on the blueprints. This will give us milestones and vantage points to view at times to be able to make moderate changes if necessary and access the situation to speed up the process if need be or factor in other elements that will build successful. The red pencil must rest on the Blueprint. I will summarize the rest of these point later but for now let us move on to our Jewels.

Jewel 265. We will never fully understand ourselves, the mystery that's buried and hid beneath the surface of who we are is the reflection of the mystery that unfolds around us each day. We can only glimpse at layers of ourselves as life reveals Its' meaning. Who are you? This question will remain in part a mystery until the day we pass form, and only what people are told, and witness is half the story. Some people are monsters, and as I witness in prison that there were people inside that the sick and derange had ostracized and have nothing to do with. For an example rapist that raped under aged handicap children, and then try to kill them. No one wants to affiliate with such a beast. We learn from ourselves if we don't take an aggressive approach by process of elimination. Who we are remains to be seen all around us, and if we develop the stomach for it what we around changes us into it, and then we become? If the environment is too horrific then that means that we are not built for such an environment and who we are may not be prone to violence, hatred and a crime related mentality. As layer of life peel back who we are, the revelation can be disturbing and quite honestly the findings could be the most traumatic thing that we have faced in our lives, good or bad.

Jewel 266. As people we take chances when we open ourselves up to new people. A month from now they can your best friend. Next year that same person they can be your worst enemy, never-the-less what is needful above all is to understand the reason and why the connection was made, then track down the purpose. This is one prime example of how the experience can be our best teacher, in terms how we invite these guest in our lives and then they get to hanging around and make themselves at home. It is only a matter of time before they drink out of the carton and leave the refrigerator door open when you are not looking to rummage through a cabinet to find something else to stick their filthy hands on. The moral of this picture is that you was the one invited them in and rather you knowingly or unknowingly that they would take over the house you invited them in, it is important that while they are there that you learn from the bastard and never give those at your door next time a second look when you slam the door in their faces. The connection on the other hand could be good and that's the chances we take in life risking the good or bad. Always give those that showed potential a chance, but in my experience, I will never pick up a strange man alongside the road. Women should only pick up women, and as far as men go, we should figure it out or parish alongside the road, but we can never put the next man in danger because we ourselves showed no threat.

Jewel 267. To be optimistic in difficulty is to show spirit to rise beyond current circumstances. Every problem has opportunities, and this gives us reason to hope. The true message of hope is when everything seems bleak that you find something good in the darkness that can be used to escape to the light. Optimism is the shear belief that it can never go completely wrong. I can only imagine with misery in my soul for those that had to hop out of the twin towers during September 11, 2001 on that gruesome Tuesday morning had hope. Perhaps some felt being able to jump to their death rather than burn was far better than being in a plane falling out of the sky and then burn. It all depends on what the mindset forced itself to embrace in all of it optimism. Some met an early death to find themselves make peace with themselves, the world and their God which would never have ever happened if they had waited to leave silently into the night.

Jewel 268. How could we possibly know where we could end up in life, or the outcome thereof. But we are responsible for taking our lives in the right direction and have an idea by choices we make today. So, as we move forward into tomorrow, we stand a greater chance of a desired result. I have found out in life that if uncertain tragic fall upon me and I fall short of my goals I would rather find myself unable to climb a new mountain than to be cut short sliding down an old one. Life is truly indeed vicious, and very uncertain, so all that is within us we must face the fear of the unknown and move forward any way. It may be by chance that we live longer than expected and have more time to enjoy the fruits of our labor the regrets of our laziness. If we are at least headed in the right direction no one can be upset about which way, we were going and if we will end up where we claim we are going.

Jewel 269. You cannot achieve or control your way to safety in life, the only thing that can be done is make peace that life is fragile, uncertain, and to be took as it comes one day at a time. Prison taught me to never take one breath for granted, because each one is leading up to the unequivocal moment of our last. We should be at peace with our last breath and embrace it with honor that we have had so many more than others that have been long gone before us. We should never be in a rush to leave because our purpose is destined with or without our consent to prove our being here. It could be to the next person to not take their life for granted or to prove to the next purpose all they can do with a life by the example of the life you lived.

Jewel 270. Happiness is here today, gone tomorrow, we embrace it, but we cannot capture it, neither can we create a recipe for achieving happiness. All we can do is maintain a sense of inner peace and joy by knowing you're living a meaningful life, even when you're not having a particularly good day. It is possible to be completely miserable and have a smile on your face. Today is uncertain, and have so many crossroads, winds and turns, that we sometimes don't know where the end will come out to be. Also, in the mist of happiness there can be a settlement of discouragement and negativity. The peace that we gain from being grateful is knowing that each day we wake up is another day above ground. The peace in life is knowing that you have done all that you know to do and are capable of and be happy with it. The true meaning of life is being humble and knowing all that you must accomplish in life has a definite meaning.

Jewel 271. In the quest of life, searching ourselves, we may never find what we have expected. That would only prove that we've known ourselves all along. What we find will be surprising and may never crossed our minds it was there. It could come in a surprise visit, similar to someone trying to harm your small infant daughter, or threaten your own life, and what you may have to become in order to survive may be alarming to even you when the blood, sweat and tears dry up, it may be that you may be a little embarrassed to look in the mirror at what you are able to become.

Some find themselves on the road of prostitution, drugs that lead to other events that may not ever been able to stomach before the drugs, so on and so forth. Like soldiers that train in the army to go to battle and preparing to rise to the occasion of their full potential and not knowing what that may fully look like, may require regular visits to the psychic for PTSD. The last thing that can be discover about ourselves that we wrestle with alone is that we may or may not know is our true limitations. Some test these boundaries with sexuality and discover that they are more drawn to the same sex or know for sure that they love the opposite or both. For the record, a person has the right to do whatever he or she wants to do with their own body besides kill or harm it. I find that I love the opposite sex and my limitations are free to experience and explore only with that nature.

Jewel 272. It is no excuse to commit a crime unless your life is at stake. If you have exhausted all legal remedies, social systems can no longer help for the purpose of survival. Then it may be true to say that your hands were forced. Duration is a word used in the practice of law when someone was forced to commit a crime, with their life being threating if they don't cooperate. The same goes for a person that may have a gun pointed to his head in various ways and not able to get clean out of the situation. The fuzzy area comes in when you can get away and call for help, and rather than do so, you go back commit the crime. In my analysis I believe that under certain circumstances when the time comes to do what is right, it is the only choice which could be a criminal act. Stealing food and medicine to give to a sick hungry child at home when everyone else got you on hold, waiting list, or perhaps come see me tomorrow.

Jewel 273. The time is now we live in that you must be proficient in at least three things to get a decent job to do one thing. I remember trying to get my first real job in a chicken factory, they wanted me to have a diploma or a GED. This was certainly as most requirements to get at least a person that was able to complete a single task. The disciple that it takes to finish school is the same requirements that is needed to complete a job. Now a day it is critical for even the most modest job to have a diploma, some technical training, or college, and to have clean credit and background. These are just to name a few, but I'm sure that the list goes on. I find myself making requirements to those that will be in my circle and stand in my corner. Not to blackball from being an associate of mine but I simple know the depths from which I came and the heights that I must go and anyone that is along for a free ride in my life better be family that has put in enormous work like my Mother.

Jewel 274. If you perfect a skill that will fuel your dream alive, then you won't have to run after it, it will make its way to you. The skill that you have is needed by the world, and you won't have to go out and solicit it, but they will come and find you and make you an offer. Your dream has all the support that it needs if you sponsor it through your skills that you develop and line up with what it is that your dream is. The skill or craft that you will perfect requires about 10,000 hrs. and then the flashpoint and beauty of its erection shall be glorious to the world. Your dream that you are keeping alive is depended upon what you are willing to learn to do to bring it to life.

Jewel 275. To have a dispute with someone and stop talking to each other is not the end of the world, but just because you have a breakdown in communication, doesn't mean you should have a break down in character. Never change who you are, when others change around you. Someone that I was very close with in prison, bald head Claudius Grayson, My homeboy and brother from another mother. Our dispute over God Knows what it was all about, but we stop speaking for about 2 or 3 weeks. That was the longest 2-3 weeks of our lives. And when the silence was over man it was a breath of fresh air, even when we could mumble back to each other and speak when we had no choice because we were on locked down. He knew I didn't have a lot of money so when he passes me a cake, I knew I didn't have to pay him back with interest like everyone else because he was the store man. By the way some people lifelong goal in life is to grow up go to prison and become the store man. I've been told that it's a great feeling of power and endearment from others. The tension was so thick in the air that you could have cut it with a knife. He usually would just knock people out that he didn't like, but we never thought of harming one another, only respect each other during our time of trying to figure out what was our problem with each other. It may have been we just needed a break from each other. After about three weeks we got it together, but we never changed into animals or anything but love and respect for each other. My Brother from another Mother Claudius Reginald Grayson.

Jewel 276. A small bump in the road may test friendship, but it should never destroy it, for one to say that it only proves they weren't friends anyway, even if they were trying really hard to become friends. All things are tested, like coals to diamond and some things by fire, like friendship. Friends are like family, when the bond is set then where else can you turn even if it's to the one that is causing the problem. Friendship is mostly tested early for the bumps in the road to determine the long Gevity of the relationship. It is too often that because people search out for friendship so desperately, that they overlook the signs that spells out that he or she is or never will be your friend. Try as you must friendship has to have the same chemistry as a marriage, and it can't be broken as easily as a few arguments and a fist fight.

Jewel 277. The man who advances himself the furthest is the one who stays ahead of himself the farthest mentally. In order to be successful, we first must book all our time with a 10% gap of leisure and family. We set the epic perpetual plan in motion willing to invite guest into our scheme and measure out how long they can stay there before they begin to cause disruption. When we get ahead of ourselves it's not a bad thing, it's only knowing what comes next and being able to be prepare for the next moment. The greater the preparation is the more likely the success of the intermediate goal that will come to create the beginning of another goal, plan of accomplishment and implementation. When you know these things while others wing it in the morning when they wake up year after year, whether they know it or not they fall further behind while you drastically distance yourself between them moving ahead.

Jewel 278. Most people become friends out of convenience rather than conviction. It is no right or wrong way to become friends in my opinion. It must be done in the spirit of truth, because rather you were pursuing an individual in a relationship or got trapped in the elevator together for a while, it is sure that truth must be at the forefront. The convenience of having a friend that is already in a career that you are pursuing may be a bit bias but, to look at someone that is coming down the hallway and say I want that to be my friend and pursue that individual as such is more conviction than convenience.

Jewel 279. A man or women's child is the best of them and the worst of them at the same time. Genetics and family background play such a major role in the character that we pass down from generation to generation. Especially when we look like the individual, and sound alike and do some of the same noticeable things, then the kid will inheritably want to impress upon themselves by doing what the parents do first before they find their own narrative. Parents pass down everything and it's up to the child to find the reason to control and temper what they are going to synthesize in their very own lives.\

Jewel 280. There is not a single person that has been shut behind the musky gates of prison and not been driven mad. The only difference between the one that continues to return back and forth into prison in a state of madness, and the one that returns to society to stay in a state of genius is control. If this genius mind that experienced madness returns to society and then close the mental gates of his mind into a prison of obedience, not only will he remain free in society, but he will be very successful. Are we all just a little bit crazy? Some have embraced poverty as a way of life because of whatever social dynamics they face and have come to realize the inevitable. Then there are other that say to live like that, they must think I'm crazy and go on to sale drugs commit crimes and so on and so forth. This could be true for a lot of reason, why people do what they do but self-control and discipline will be at the top of every conversation that lures people to do the right thing or the wrong. It is prison either way people look at it and they say give me prison or give me death. Liberty and Freedom is a dream that has never really be clarified without some type of control on the end. The truth of the matter is what prison is more desirable, as I went to the FED's and people thought that I was in a far better prison than the state prison. It was all captivating to me; therefore, I saw no real difference. I learned a lot of freedoms where just the illusion and byproduct of society and controls that in the end lead to prison if you didn't understand how liberties worked. When you commit to go through the gates of control that will lead to success then, those things that will lead to prison are no longer available for consumption. You're focused and locked in.

Jewel 281. Chains and Freedom goes hand and hand for you can not have one without the other. The only freedom that we have is to choose what controls are we going to succumb to, and even then it depends on where you are born at in the world because the prison of the mind will ravish all of your hopes and dreams in some demographic and only want what you are told you want. How can I want only one wife if it's so many women available? It's because we are told from childhood up that we should only be in relationship with one woman or man, while other culture say you can have as many as you can afford. We are only servant to what we are exposed to and that which we don't know.

Into the Sweets
Dedicated: R.I.P Laurence Brown

The epic streets, were virtual reality scenes
seen sights still stuck in my head

Traumatized, by what never caught my eyes but,
imagined screams of Laurence dead

The epic seas sought him, after cries and
tears from Timmy his brother shed

Me and Deet my best friend for years, also kin
to me on my mother side and dad.

I was led by him in the concrete jungle, hid
from his mother Noisy under his bed

She said I was trouble and needed to be
beat, and I agreed that I was dread

We got around everywhere on feet, I miss
his sister Keshia and brother Ced

I would raid the cookie jar then eat up all the
boiled sausages without the bread

I'm rarely home and they fed good at Noisy
house, so I'll eat their instead

Crimes printed in the papers, capers we had
pulled off, the next day we read

His gold teeth are thanks to me, me and Deet
stood together in adversity and bleed.

What epic skies we must rise to, to tell of
two guy and the life we had to tread

Life is like a bowl of chocolates, just don't get
caught when you enter into the sweets.

By: Marvin Thomas.

Jewel 282. There is no right way to do the wrong thing. Situations and insinuated circumstances make people change, their drive, the determination and what path that they may have been on. Some believe that even in the wrong situation that they can become resourceful and creative and have reason to do this wrong thing by some right method. It's like thinking that you can judge, and convict all on your own thinking. It's nothing in completely being right that has a once of wrong in it, it's only that we must make peace with ourselves that if it's done in this manner that it was no other way.

Jewel 283. While biting your fingernails may be sure sign of nervousness or lack of confidence, the most dangerous sign it proves is a lack of discipline and self-control. What time can we be taking advantage of during the time that we are biting our fingernails or some other time-wasting measure, we could be doing something much more productive. When we know something is not right and we do it anyway then this is a tell sign that our discipline is not there.

Jewel 284. A woman with a dirty mouth and hygiene unkept to the point of awful breath is also sure to be found with an unclean vagina. And an elite man to notice this and still have sex with her is foolish and not what he claims to be. The truth is that when you have no power over the temptation of a sexual urge, then this will prevent you from being a person of an elite status. We must be sure that people that we deal with are judged from top to bottom and some things that are seen give away to things that are not seen about the person. When the things that people can see about us are not presentable then you can rest assure the things that are not seen are disgusting.

Jewel 285. A great orator not only plant ideas effectively into the audience to be grasped and claimed as their very own, the orator must also embrace the ideas of the audience as his own and mirror themselves. The power of orators is being able to speak to their self. When you speak to an audience especially with passion and conviction it is those that are among the greats are those that in their minds don't see those that are before them only himself. Speaking to yourself on a regular basis gives you the practice you need to find out what may be conceptualized by someone else.

Jewel 286. The elite always can detect ignorance from a far; all that is done is to capture a glimpse of the mental hygiene which is never kept up to par. For the ignorant will rarely bathe in wisdom, and the voice of their reason smells awful. The destructive monster of today's society is ignorance, and it has tell tell signs all around it. The result of what we are has a way of smelling where we been, leaving smudge marks on our hands and leave footprints everywhere we go. Those that know and walk the way of the wise demand to understand what they may face or encounter up the road. These features are just a few examples of when foolish people speak, they are bound to slip up and say something foolish much more than someone that has emerged himself in the hall of disciplined wisdom.

Jewel 287. Even an enemy must be treated well and with respect when both parties have the same interest and are able to conduct business that profit you. It is necessary that in the field of business in order to thrive you must have mutual respect and have a common goal. To like one another has never been on the list. In fact, it has never been really stated that you must be friends. The enemy of my enemy is my friend and if its poverty that is your true enemy for example if it's in business then the common goal is money and not to hate someone.

Jewel 288. The two emotions that dominates the thinking of a man when it comes to failure, is the fear to fail; and or the fear to succeed. Failure will always be apart of your life so we must fail forward. The most successful man in the world, deals with failure positively, by allowing it to dominate why he must succeed, while the individual who has not been able to imagine success yet allows failure to dominate with fear of all that he or she will encounter in order to succeed.

Jewel 289. Sleep is a close friend to learning. When sleep comes into our lives it's no more to give us the refueling that we need in order to give it a go again the next day. When these two links up learning and sleep, they will begin to work in unison, and perfect rotation. The power nap is something that we have heard by some to measure the success they're of who need but little of it because they have much to do. The truth of the matter is that when you are well rested no matter what, it will put you in the perfect mindset to learning and recovering the information that you have already took in.

Jewel 290. A man that says he's madly in love with a woman, then turn around and lie down naked, and let another woman sit upon him and latch on to draw out his virtue which is sacred for his woman alone is crazy. This mad man is no better than a rabid minded dog that will poke and run behind anything. Such a man is not a man and deserves to be treated ill and even some cases put down like a wild animal. This is the reality that our generation faces on a consistent basis, of infidelity. Some relationships in this day and time have what they call an open relationship which have rules that are not contemporary and liberal. In fact, they are quite the contrary, relationships in this day and time have come with vulgarity and indecency. Being able to sleep, with whoever as long as the other partner knows them, or some I've heard of couples having the rules of wearing protection was the only limitation, and a lady told me once that her man didn't mind her sleeping around as long as she didn't do it outside of her race. The measurements of what agreements are right or wrong are up to the couple but, I say that when you have the intense love for a woman, then you will almost always consider her feeling before you consider your own.

Jewel 291. It should make a man sick to the stomach to think about having sex with another woman once he has fallen in love. This is the true nature of love; it will always cling to that which it loves and not want to abandon that for some unknown encounter. Can a man love more than one woman, as in the days of old and biblical? My answer is said how can you have two masters for you will love one and hate the other. It is a fine line between love and hate, and if I had the opportunity to choose which I could have multiple women or just one. I would say I would pick the one which composes all my favorite characteristics.

Jewel 292. To know that you can rise beyond your present circumstance in thought is well, but to commit action upon every decision as if you have already risen is greatness. This is the essences of success, the belief that you have everything that you need to make what you see as success come to pass. If your present circumstance is dark and diminished and you know to be able to move forward is to have a flashlight. Then you realize that you have a flashlight in you backpack then the movie can go off and show the credits. The same is with this jewel, every movement now after coming into the knowledge of the how will be execution of every action afterwards. Moving with precision and calculation.

Jewel 293. Always fight for each moment to live even if its only to die the next day. Life is precious and the moments that we share with each other are so detrimental. It could be that fighting for a particular moment in life and after achieving that moment will grant others a much more valuable outlook on life if day in and day out, we fulfil our purpose. It is possible to pass on a mindset of a high achiever when you believe that each moment has its purpose and it must be fulfilled.

Jewel 294. God has a divine plan for each person. Our purpose is strongly mixed with people we come in contact with every day. So, take care to search everyone in spirit and in truth. They may have keys to your destiny. This is one of my favorite Jewels because it has the sense of purpose with not only us but for others. Your breakthrough may be locked into someone else. It is also necessary to know that we have to make investment into others because we don't know what all your life will be, and to maximize your life you may have to bring someone else to their best use, so that they can give you what you need to invest into yourself. I have what millions of people, in terms of hope, belief and presenting the tools to this chaotic world, that men and women can be effective. I'm just a few people at this moment from getting it to you, and I've came thousands of miles and met thousands of people to get to that one.

Jewel 295. People who are popular have the pressures to remain, while those who blend in and go undetected are at ease to be themselves. Strive to be in between well known but not liked by everyone and never get caught up becoming someone else. This is clearly the mindset to have to be able to not have targets on you or having to be so scrutinized that all that you do is under a microscope. This is ok if you are confident that either way you are constantly yourself. The pressure of this can run off track and out of control. Lastly, it is our most confident moment in life that when our reasoning's are questioned and our motives are judge that we can look to ourselves in the mirror and still recognize what it is that we are called to do.

Jewel 296. The moment a woman or man lies to their significant other is the exact moment they begin to kill the relationship. Without trust love is dead. It is often questioned when is the exact moment that the relationship is finally over. I say that it is the moment that you are willing to sacrifice the principle and values of that relationship for selfish gains. It could be drinking, drugs, or another person. The lie is just the image of what can be seen and measured in the physical to represent the time of the exact moment.

Jewel 297. We are enticed by the world to be great, despite our present condition. True greatness already lies entrenched in us. Our only challenge is to find the great counterpart on the other side that will reveal itself within us. Some of my counterparts have been Eric Thomas, Les Brown and Jim Rohn which are all motivational speakers, Nikki Giovanni, Langston Hughes, and Robert Frost are all Poets. Lastly, Martin Luther King Jr., Henry Ford, and Steve Jobs are all businessmen and major influencers of the world. This alone seeing what some of these greats have done makes it impossible not to want to be apart of something great, even if you must sacrifice your life to obtain it. Meaning the life, you would live, with friends, and leisure time will be replaced with hard work no friends and a lot of pressure to complete task, goals and objectives. My greatest counterpart was my wife who showed me myself and dug inside deep to the core of me to find my excellence.

Jewel 298. Living for the moment is good and bad. It is good to enjoy each moment as if it was your last, because one day it will be. The bad on the other hand when you don't enjoy the moment preparing for the next because you'll never be happy. Much will a person will leave undone, so be happy for the moment and cautious of what actions you take will affect tomorrow no matter if it never comes. The lives we chose and the hand we are dealt are often so distant from what it is that we want out of life. To make peace with this we must enjoy the simple things in life and make sure that the time we have here on earth are good moments as much as possible. Then happiness becomes a factor and what is it that we like to do, because when we find out what that thing is, we need to spend the rest of our lives going after it. We are unable to fulfill all our hopes in dreams on the flip side, so we must sip and eat slices of the colossal dreams that we intend to pursue. Knowing every step in this direction is the right direction and is what we chose. We don't need to focus on the time we lost, in trying to figure out what it was that we wanted.

Jewel 299. Successful people seldom have time to eat, drink, sleep or use the bathroom unless they are getting paid for it at the same time. It can be seen in the lives of celebrities where even the clothes they wear are model and endorsed. Jewelry are given to them through contracts to wear during certain times and foods and drinks are also promoted on camera. Time is always stringent and when you finally have time to sleep, rather on planes or in outside campers before some presentation, they are still on the clock.

Jewel 300. One must be very aggressive in the financial world to land on top. While making money you must also make more money. This reminds me of a commercial that has an actor in it. The company is paying the actor to do the commercial, then he has endorsers to promote their brand through the actor whether it's clothes or a soft drink. Lastly, while on set gets paid again for doing interviews and selling exclusive bloopers on the side.

Jewel 301. No one happens to be successful all of a sudden, she must have strong work ethics. No one stumbles upon greatness, even though it is right in front of our faces, it must be carefully crept upon and apprehend like a butterfly. The work ethics represents the discipline and commitment level it takes, the patience that is required to come upon greatness, and only a few men have been able to walk right up to it and grab a hold of it, and the key word keep it.

Jewel 302. Never ask a bum how to become a millionaire. True story, I gentleman came up to me today, and he wasn't dressed horrible and he spoke of some professionalism. I was working a kiosk at the Battlefield Mall. The kiosk is a virtual reality game system. The man I found out was name Marvin too. He ask me would I consider selling the machine that I was operating at the time which the actually owner wanted to sale at a price of $5,500. I told him the price and he said let me get his number to call and speak with him. I had two old phones laying on my desk, where I tried to sale them and couldn't get a dime for them. The man went on to ask me whose phones where they, I told him mine, He ask me could I donate them to him for money for his coffee shop. My response was you come to me and tell me that you are going to open up a coffee shop and that you wanted to buy the VR machines, and in the second breath ask me to give you wanted two worthless phones as a donation for your business. Then came back later after I gave him the phone and ask could he get my name and number so he could collect donations for his business at my kiosk. This is the most insane mindset I've ran across all month. You can not ask to buy in one sentence and in the next beg. This does not make sense and this is the mind set of the bum. Even if he has made millions in his life, and says that being a bum makes him happier. I firmly believe that this is not true. The truth is being a bum is easier and nowhere in the mind of a potential millionaire should he be exposed to such foolishness as a method or teaching.

Jewel 303. Do not be afraid of temptation, in fact face it head on with a courageous stare, and with all of your wits figure out how to escape this which is bound to happen if you fall victim. What some live by is whatever is going to happen is going to happen so the best thing to do is to have a great attitude. This is the mindset to have with confidence, that you are able to defeat any obstacles, and when these obstacles come, don't look away because it will only give that thing which is trying to intimidate you more power, and that maybe the only edge that is needed to defeat you. Not only stare it in the eyes, but begin summoning the urged to run towards. Never look for temptation but let it not change your courageous attitude to move forward.

Jewel 304. Keep an inspirational song in your heart for times of despair. You will most certainly need it's especially when trying to rise to the top. The songs that we hold in our hearts are the little trivets that keep us going even in the moments of hopelessness. When we have certain Jewels in our heart, or a tiny little song that we can see when the moment of truth comes, it will get us by.

The inspiration and the hope is our future, because this in the bank emotion will come in handy when most needed.

Jewel 305. It is not enough to do all you can and have not accomplished your goal. Even a millionaire will beg and borrow to accomplish his goal of making billions. The secrets is when you've done all you can do, then it's time to start begging for help. Every day is the moment of truth, when you are on the higher path and trying to accomplish some goal that is not attainable to all. We must refresh ourselves with self-development measures and keep focus constantly. Doing all we can do is a relentless grind, that will wear out the most enthusiastic and motivated. Yet that's not the end of our troubles, those that are on the same path as we are, we risk the loss of help, loved ones, and, definitely the loss of money. To say we lost everything and still have our lives in terms of accomplishing some of our goal is a very lazy thing to say.

Jewel 306. Success and preparation goes hand and hand, in fact the most prepared people sustain the longest when things that make us fail, come upon us. If we know these things will always come and prepare for it then, success can out last the failure. Even when we are successful, things are always coming upon us that are silhouettes of failure. Failure constantly thrown even at the most successful person will make him crumble. Failing circumstances came upon successful actors like Brittany Murphy, athletes like Mike Tyson and Michael Jackson. The only way to ward off such negative influences are to create fail safe systems that act as a safety net at the very appearance of failure.

Jewel 307. We must respond in life with a sense of urgency and desperation when it comes to accomplishing our dreams and ambitions, like one that lie on a death bed with a second chance to get up. Life the one shot deal of all of our experiences must be taking very serious. Those of us that are lucky in our failure at life will get a chance hopefully at a ripe old age to sit in a rocking chair or wheel chair and reminisce in regret. When young we must take but little time to say what it is that we will accomplish because the truth of the matter is that it may take the rest of our natural lives going after it. Facts also remains that even when it takes longer than we anticipate in getting our goals and dreams accomplished that we must hold firm to our commitment and know that once we empower the will to do something the only thing that is left is the full vision of it's manifestation.

Jewel 308. We must be ready for the future when it comes. And prevent finding ourselves in positions that when it arrives we don't know what to expect. The art of planning and time management will help us know the future a bit more. We should never walk into a day that has no vision at all, this could be very dangerous and when anything lapse, your quick judgment may not help you in situation. We can't prevent if death awaits us around the next corner of the day, but if it's anything that we can do to prevent a horrible accident by having made plans that are checked for mishaps and accidents, then it will suit you to do so. Write out what it is that you will do for that day on a sheet of paper that pertains to your goals. Fill out the calendars with these ambitions, from day to day, week to week, from year to year.

Jewel 309. Success is bigger than a 7 letter word, but it will always be meaningless until each individual utilize the letter I and place it at the front. This is the natural order of things, when success is a factor it can do nothing alone unless it has a I similar to a suffix. I gives this word power and inspiration. It is like an inhibitor that will rest upon a person. Success is like a trench coat with double insinuation, hanging in the closet, but on that cold day, until I get into it. Then I will be successful.

Jewel 310. Some women have no need for love, romance and fairy tales. Now a days women position themselves for power, prestige, and wealth. They have lost faith and their focus is on delivering the fairy tale to themselves. Our generation has become very independent from women empowerment. So many men have sold dreams and fairy tales at the cost of so many lives that was lived out, hard and much struggle. Women seeing mothers, sisters, and daughters buying into the knight in white shiny armor, believe that it was all fool's gold, and want to give it a shot. A lot of women don't mind taking care of a man she loves and knows loves her, but to waste her life in want, will never forgive herself or him if she don't do all she can to get what she believes she is worth or deserves.

Jewel 311. A secret that is untold can be harmless and innocent, but to try to cover it up is sneaky, divisive and a betrayal to those who long to know the truth. With this being said we must be able to quickly say to those that know detrimental information to not say a word if when they find out, will cause even bigger confusion. This can be also said that ignorance is bliss, and to not know is better than knowing and can't do anything about it. The moment we receive information it begins to burn us up to deliver it to sources that will within us make us validated to be able to have knowledge of certain information.

Jewel 312. People are blind when trying to lean success on spiritual attributes. One is not necessarily successful because he is spiritual or prays. However, having seen so many with a form of success and are not spiritual make me believe so. But, to be both spiritual and successful in my opinion, it is better, just not necessary. This is in my life experiences the great conundrum. There are very wicked people that are enjoying all of the spices of life at the expense and happiness of innocent people that are living honest, spiritual and trying everyday to do the right thing. We say from a spiritual point that their wealth is laid up for us and it will be restored to the righteous. Some see this as only after we are dead and that we may be believing in some form of fantasy, imagination or false hope to keep us from turning as wicked as they are. This religious backdrop was even said to be created by wicked men to be able to keep the righteous calm in doing the things to keep them wealthy. I'm not sure how to process all of what I've exposed to you because if I am a wealthy righteous man, will someone more righteous inherit my wealth and call me wicked because I didn't feed every poor person that I ran across. This conundrum is to me a reward that dangles in front of us to give us hope and to justify the reason one stays righteous. My last thoughts is if you can get success, wealth, and happiness and peace of mind all at the same time, devise a plan and spend the rest of your natural life going after it.

Jewel 313. The idea that bringing forth success must be nurtured, protected and cared for like a baby, and when it has matured with feeling it all, the inspiration and skill set it takes to survive, then it will accomplish that which it purposed. The idea of success being a baby only is used to represent that it has to have attributes like an infant to be respected properly. Very few have success on their mind 24/7 until someone that is more successful than they are walk passes and this becomes their reminder. The truth of the matter is that we all know that becoming successful is hard grueling work like hanging chickens in a chicken factory for the slaughter. You have to first have the stomach for the eerie smell, the tremendous amounts of blood, and the noise of all of the screams and cries of chickens being shocked then dipped in scowling hot water to have their throats slit and then the real madness of the operation begins. We having even spoke about the endless never stopping lines that fly pass with the expectations of two chicken feet will be pulled off the belt by two guys in so much safety gear that he can barely move to hang these chickens at rapid speeds. I called that part of my life a wicked nightmare. I see the episodes replay again when I started embarking on the road to success, it's hard, grueling, and painful. With the protection of the idea that has been picked up and wrapped up and to be cared for no matter what is the determination.

Jewel 314. Sometimes it pays to be in the right place at the right time and many have made fortunes off of dumb luck. Quick story, when I was very young, there was a young girl that I like that had a special manipulation tactic that she used. I helped her move and afterwards I found myself becoming friends with her and I would put furniture together for her or bring things by for her. She had a boyfriend and I became the shoulder to lean on but she was very adamant on her position not to cheat on him and we could only further our relationship if she broke up with him. I had tried all I could do to sway her that if he made her cry that often that she should give me a chance. I was in the right place at the right time to further the relationship had I stayed in the moment. After time went by of me running back and forth to her house only to be a damp shoulder, I became discouraged, and I grew weary. It was the very next phone call that had haunted me throughout a large period of my adolescence, that when she called I didn't answer and I refuse to go over. This call I found out quite sometime later that it was the one that I spent all those months waiting on. She told me that she had dumped her boyfriend and called with intentions to reward me for all those days that I was that shoulder. I was in the right place at the right time, but my timing was a little off and that why when we fall in these positions we must wait out the desired outcome. Every once and awhile you get lucky with money like this too.

Jewel 315. The rich and wealthy 90% of the time believe that the reason for the poor is because of laziness and inability to be capable of possessing the skills to obtain wealth. The poor believe 90% of the rich and wealthy has obtained it by ruthlessness and a maniac drive of determination these assumption in part are both true, but who we are connected with and in relationships with is the others 10% which is the bigger part. The rich very seldom worry about what the poor is doing because they don't contribute to their cause. Why do the poor worry themselves about what the rich is doing, this is pathetic, and shows the inferiority between the rich and the poor. While the rich is making their dreams come true, the poor sit back and watch and live vicariously through the eyes of the rich. In closing, when we are at our happiest, no matter how rich or how poor, it is through the people we know and share a bond with.

Jewel 316. Sometimes we can work endlessly to become something that we are not and never will become, and then there are times without effort become something that others never could hope to obtain. This is all about the gift that is within us and what we must do to be what our purpose and destiny is. Those attributes are in use from youth up and for an example if we are good with numbers as a kid but we find jobs in writing and drawing, then we may work many hours trying to write books and journals when our gift may be an engineer.

Jewel 317. It is only certain what we are, till one day we accidently stumble into it. We only know the moment what we have become, when we have become that, and our confidence can't fall into question by Jesus Christ himself. It can't be shaken by ourselves, or without doubt anyone that knows us wonder what we are. We stumble upon ourselves when we see who we are from this other side of the mirror of glasses in our eyes. We then begin to fantasize about this image we've seen and begin to walk, talk and becoming that individual inversely and subconsciously.

Jewel 318. If I'm giving you criticism and you get upset that's fine, you shouldn't love me any more or less, perhaps more but if you love me less or no more then perhaps you never loved me at all. The correction of our behavior, principles, values, or any other area that can be criticized is not a death warrant for a relationship. Love is immortal and has no expiration date. This is the true nature of love.

Jewel 319. To accomplish a goal that is detrimental it is best to map out the goal step by step then proceed forward as if you was made to do it with a gun pointed to the back of your head. This is probably the only way to accomplish a goal is to act as if someone is pointing a gun to the back of your head. Very seldom are we highly motivated to do that which will benefit ourselves. We must be coerced, manipulated, or bullied into doing the right thing for ourselves concerning accomplishing goals and ambitions. Sometimes we must be coned into doing that which we must do.

Jewel 320. In business one must be smart and ruthless, in ways to build the base and create friends on both side of customers and vendors and then when one is strong enough must have the guts to cut any and everyone to stay alive as in desperation and on a last leg. The true nature of business is to have little to know feelings on ethics in such a way that if your mom is working for you and she can't perform, do you fire her? NO! But you give her a more able job that she can do, and this is just business. Businesses can seem rude or insensible but in all reality it's all about x's and o's and making sure that the business is able to survive no matter what, sometimes friends and family get cut, customers that spend good money but are bad business, and other business associates that may have started from day one, but did not grow with the company to serve the needs of what it is that the business is trying to accomplish.

Jewel 321. To stay current in these days and ages one must be able to take advantage of the future in predictions such as technology or the next best thing. Then it is possible to be relevant. It is very few people or environments that exist in the future, most always get hand me down, fashion, technology, and even principles and values. To live in the future means that you are on whatever it is that is about to be released to the public during the time the rich and military have it. To know about products before they are released and have them is to stay relevant in today's time. To have them when they hit shelves is to fall behind today's time and perhaps into oblivion.

Jewel 322. Most of the world that are poor walk over thousands of dollars seen as trash, millions of dollars of fresh ideas and people that was over looked that had billions for you to invest in you, all to chase down a dollar blowing in the wind. This horrific truth is a matter of little to no imagination. When we see the money already formed it stems from an idea that has already be produced, when most get the dollar that is not even worth a dollar in current days because of inflation, and the value of everything depreciates so when it's said and done you may have about 40 cent. The poor in mind with ideas of who to contribute with their lives is the basis of never really accumulating wealth needed to sustain major blows like a down economy, downsizing, or just plain you're fired.

Jewel 323. Never put yourself in a position that you have to borrow money from your enemy, because he may just lend it to you; but with a price that will make you vulnerable and susceptible to attack. The saying goes that if you are at the mercy of someone that has to lend you something make sure that it's from someone that has the most to benefit from you paying them back. It is in more cases then we know that when you have come to borrow money from someone it was right on time, because the life of money has to continue to rotate and cycle into more money, so think not that someone you know is smart by just sitting on money. This is the ways of the unwise. The wise keep their money in the hands of those that need it so bad that they will pay almost double to use it.

Jewel 324. Not to have a dream is irresponsible and disrespectful. It should be a shame to not make a contribution to the planet that we were birth into and only take and exploit all that we came into contact with. The embarrassment lies down with us when we close our eyes and hauled off into the grave when so many have risked their lives and dedicated their lives so that we could find a better way. We settled for what they accomplish and marveled at the sights that where already here and never gave a second thought to what could have become.

The Paige in the Lost Book

The Paige's flipping in fleeting winds brought
the being of this beautiful book alive

It began to thrive like a living soul and it serenaded
musicians to come from far and near

Ohh what do we have here, a violinist came to
stroke the hair of the violin with her bow

The vibes were so gyrated in rhythm, bass pounding
in the hole and working in unison.

These two instruments were sent by some Goddess
to play out lives we live in the book

But on second look, there was something missing
and the violinist could no longer strum

A Paige was gone, so the Paige's stop turning with
the winds, yet the music had charms

Then out the clear storm the Paige came along
and it also was a beautiful being all alone

Paige expressed emotions deep as the ocean, and
the book and Paige played with each other.

From back to cover they explored each other, not
allowing the flesh or bone to smother

These two beautiful beings with no wind sent
Paige into a frenzy and got wet as sin

And to protect Paige the cover of the book got
hard as 3 hail Mary's and closed in

And then the wind blew again, and many pretended
to hear the music the violinist played

While inside of the covers of the beautiful book
of music lies the naked truth of Paige

BY: Marvin Thomas

Jewel 325. Two ways to interpret what you see is eye sight and mind sight, eye sight is only being able to go off what you see. Mind sight is to not physically see it but behold it in your mind. This is said to hone in on creative vision in the mind means that you are able to be of good judgment and to also have insight on what people may or may not do. Its from the experiences you have everyday that will guide you into what makes since what a person will do. The truth of the matter is eye sight is the worst sight to have if you have not gained mind sight. It is said believe nothing of what you hear and half of what you see. Some times people paint pretty pictures that are awesome to the eye and behind each detail line is a vicious lie.

Jewel 326. There are only a few things that matters, find them, master them and go on to be successful. Some people think doing more is getting more done, but is quite the opposite. In fact you will get less of the things done that matters if you are working on things that do not stretch you drive you and ultimately lead you to your goals that you acknowledge you will be successful from. Only work on the important stuff, the stuff that will engage you to your hopes and dreams.

Jewel 327. In the secret to becoming a millionaire, you first have to become a hundredaire, and then a thousandaire, and with those two accomplishments alone and achieving those millstones with the experience of saving, investing, and having multiple sources of income coming in, a millionaire status will be obtained with a surety. The basic principle stands with every man and woman that has the same 24 hours in a day to do what the next man or woman has. The shared experience that every millionaire identifies with is being able to master the ability to save, invest with multiple streams of income for a period sometimes stretching for years, before the flash-point takes over and money comes in from every which away. The value system is the same also, to spend very stringent and accumulate as if you was broke and without a source of wealth.

Jewel 328. Don't inspire to be married or motivated to find a women to be with, yet be inspired to die married to that woman the motivation should be the end result of what you hope to acquire. It is in a person mind always to see only what they want to see in obtaining the things that they want. It should never be the focus that keeps us motivated, but look at that thing we want as if we already have it, and then focus on how to maintain it after it gets into our grasp. Tell people when you are broke, that I'm going for it, they will quite naturally say what? Then you tell them millions of dollars to be able to reshape the position of my current family and down future generations. This will give a greater impact on the things that motivate you when you have a purpose for it.

Jewel 329. Change can be as sudden and drastic as going to a club today on Saturday and when you pass by on Sunday it's turned into a church. These are the great monuments of our time and since real estate is far and few, during this generation it's all about availability and what can possible work. I've actually been to a church where it was like a community building and after the class reunion was cleaned up on the Saturday night, then the Pews and Pulpit are brought in.

Jewel 330. A Man that desired the woman of his dreams and search out how will he know when he finds her will know when she turns his desires to even look at another woman. His eyes may be the only thing that moves her but as she walks by his body will be a vegetable. His look will be mild and momentarily then remembers quickly what he has in his grasp. This moment of truth is scary because this is a moment of being vulnerable and not knowing if he is the man of her dreams. Test can be done on her as well, but the most important thing to remember is to know that the body will not in any way be attracted to another woman until the mind release the signal it's free to search elsewhere.

Jewel 331. Ignorance and fear are twin sister and you can usually find them both in bed seducing a black man. This is a very powerful quote because, the truth of the matter is that as black men we fall victim of fear and ignorance as quickly as a woman. The ignorance of being able to build a community to thrive in verses one to destroy are just some of the usually feats, and the fear of death rules us to the point that we rather be broke and die of old age than to take a chance to have fun live free and financially stable and die young. We are all going to die regardless of if we tip toe around on earth or if we wildly go after the things we want, and hunt them down till we get them. It is hard to tell them from one another because it is ignorant to be fearful and to be fearful is ignorant and they both have no real power over you unless you give it power. I can say they are both very expensive and will eventually cost us our lives anyway.

Jewel 332. It is knowledge that mix with consistent honest work ethic, tend to soak the mind of an ignorant foolish man like a deer. When the wildness is soaked out he will be then clear minded and ready to change the world. The self-development must start with purging and a sense of cleaning. Going back and tracking mistakes and in revelation discovering what has not worked so far are good reflections. Then after some time of clear thought, it is necessary to find elements that can be brought in and introduced to the individual that will not overwhelm him, because if it does he or she may revert back to what they have only been exposed to. Then when the water of purity has sanitized them the salt which is knowledge will preserve them and bring them deeper into the future which can only be done through knowledge.

Jewel 333. Always be ready to meet a threat at the back door, when it comes in asking are you ready. Do not run back into the bedroom to warn and wake the woman and children. This is the coward way to take flight himself. Rather shush the threat as to motion to not wake the woman and children and race forward towards them without blinking and without fear and say I'm ready. The only way to tackle an obstacle is to run forward towards it, because if they came in through the back door into your environment they must have no fear, and the only way to focus on how to dominate this force is with the exact same force. Any kind of running from the direction will give that force the extra energy it needed to dominate you. Always remember this is your domain, you know where everything is and even if you cut the lights off, you should still be victorious.

Jewel 334. The difference between the way rich people think and poor people think is, if you was to offer a poor person $125 dollars on hour for the rest of his life no raise, commission, no questions, the poor would usually accept. The rich would refuse knowing it's only 24 hours in the day and this is a limitation. It

limits income that will depreciate with inflation year by year. If you accept a pay without limitation as a dollar amount per hour, then one can achieve through compiled and compound income beyond his imagination. It is true that we all have the same 24 hours as the next man and woman and many are using these hours to the fullest. It is by no small matter that when someone offers you whatever sum a money to work an hour, that the operation of that job is more than likely worth double, maybe more. This is the selling of ones services at dirt cheap, and most people sadly don't know what their skills are worth and never try to sale them to the highest bidder. It is almost impossible to find a wealthy person to trade dollar per hours, this narrow vision are adopted by those that are more laborious and find themselves on a 9 to 5 for 20 years and then look for a system to take care of them, but the retirement package isn't set up for them to live comfortable. In fact the system is wondering why are you still alive because that is why the age is being raised constantly because people are steady trying to beat the system by living longer. At the end of the day, when the rich has said and done it all, you will see the gains made by putting in not only years' worth of work into a couple of months, but the people brought on board to reproduce the same efforts will do it for so cheap that even if setbacks occur that the system of reproducing the efforts, products, service or whatever has took such a lucky leap that it just want be any bonus this year, or perhaps a 50 cent raise.

Jewel 335. Women be careful how you ask other men for help when you have a man at the house that is inadequate and unproductive in getting you the help you need. This man has just been given power by your consent to come in the relationship and prove his worth, and destiny. What little you have established is at least in harmony with who you have overseeing the relationship. On the other hand you could be creating a monster in giving this person power and within moment go from a simple favor to being out of control. This is like inviting a vampire into your house as old folklore puts it, if you don't they can do you no harm. The same goes for a man that you invite into your relationship, not saying that he will wreak havoc, but if the case is made then he sure can cause some damage. The harmony of a relationship is when no one knows what's going on inside the relationship besides the two in it. Anytime you bring some-one else in your business, then you may be asking for trouble. Never give consent for even family members to speak negative or positive of your relationship without knowing that it could have an effect on their relationship if not addressed appropriately.

Jewel 336. Show me your friends and I'll show you your future. We know that our friends are a large influence of who we are, and we would be wise to look around and see where it is that the group is going.

Jewel 337. I rather be soar from too much working out rather than too much rest. In life you are going to be in pain, and it's noth-ing but hurt from here. It is more beneficial to ache and be in pain from a development stand point, rather than be in hurt for nothing. Laying around will make your bones stiff and sore, and sleeping all the time will cause muscles to ache and pain, rather a good work out will do the same but it will give you a sense of purpose.

Jewel 338. If we don't hear the voice that motivates us clearly in our heads then it will be impossible to fulfill your dreams ambi-tions. I've always said that in order to have a clear sense of directions that you must have pictures hanging on the four corners of your mind, to visible show you which way that you must go and where you will end up at. The same is for those that have heard and sought after the voice of reason to help guide them in a world of uncertainty and inability to focus. My voice that I hear in the morning is Eric Thomas telling me to wake up and go about my day as the rest of the 1% world that I've committed myself to be a part of. I also believe that the voices of those that motivate you compels you to act and you have such respect for the people and what they have accomplished that you comply with the voice.

Jewel 339. If you are on your way to becoming the best, then the best will know that you are coming for them. They will either roll out the red carpet or attempt to recruit you to aide and assist them on their path of greatness. The truth of the matter is that what-ever arena that you dominate it will take but little time before everyone begins to talk about you. It could be in a negative way at first, but at the end of the day whoever is the best will begin to get all the attention and those that are just negative will fade away into obscurity.

The Woman and the Guitar
Dedicated to Kayla's Guilbault's Guitar

Wondering eyez mesmerized by the body
of this black instrument that lies

Synthesized musicians fingers immortalized
the strings of It's paralyzed hair

Just lying there, have you ever stared at
it and marveled at it's beauty

Ready to be played with on each note, on
tender chords steady to soothe me

The round hole in the middle harmonize
the vibes as strings are plucked in F

Strummed angel soft in the chord A, Devilishly
ferocious pricked in the key D

The ruby red rose was exposed and given
unceremoniously before the encore

Shush don't say no more, but the note had
left bread crumbs with every stroke

Or the affair the two shared as they laid
both overcome by the fleeting winds

Beating vehemently inside the instrument,
making them both rest there eyez

A tired girl cuddled with strumming fingers
in hair of a black instrument that lies

By Marvin Thomas

Jewel 340. Can you tell truly the accomplishments of a person over his life time, by the size of his tombstone or where his grave is located. Surely not is the answer. But it can be with certain that If you pull up to the library of congress you will be able to find that persons name and his life work will follow. This is the great paradox of living and trying to be recognized while alive and finding out where you will be ranked among the greats. Sadly to say this will rarely be accomplished while living. It is only after death that one will research and find out what was the life aspirations of the human being and where did they add up in our culture and life. It is only in the library of congress that you can find someone and figure out all that a person was affiliated with during his or her life time.

Jewel 341 To run from a barking dog Is foolish and ill advise, unless you are certain that it is no way to escape. Yet if you do have an escape this may be safer. This will be more fearful than running away but rather turn around and run toward the dog. The results can be alarming as when you do so it is very highly likely that the dog will run back to the yard and continue to bark from there, fearing what monster that was, that came after them. There was a time when I was young and I use to ride my bicycle passed this vicious dog. It happened on this one day as I was speeding by as normal and the crazy dog came running down behind my bike. The worst thing that could have ever happened, happened. My chain popped off and I begin to slow down. With the instincts of being petrified I hopped off the bike and hurled in into the ditch offside of the road in anger and begin to chase the dog. Something amazing happened, the dog ran back to the yard and looked on in a curious type fear, not knowing what happened to the young boy that he use to chase, and where did the monster come from on the bike.

Jewel 342. Eternity is being in the graveyard of encyclopedia. To have your name mention every now and then by current family members while they are still here is surely not what we expect while we are living the justice that we deserve. When your name is brought up for generations to come, and affiliated with learning institutions, then you are on your way to eternity. The encyclopedia where history is made a curriculum and you are a major part of that, as long as our social society stays as it is in today's time, then we can be sure that your name and the teaching of your mind will live forever.

Jewel 343. The rich buy cars and mansions while the wealthy purchases companies and real estate. Warren Buffet bought Coco-Cola and Bill Gates being the founder of Microsoft are men of great wealth. They may have the cars and mansions but it wasn't before they had purchase more companies than they could shake a stick at Dan Gilbert the owner of the Cleveland Calvirlears, at this time owns about 51 companies and the more companies you own the higher the probabilities for more mansions and cars.

Jewel 344. Success is the best revenge and aphrodisiac at the same time. Most of the time when a person gains massive success, it is for the purpose of revenge. Someone that didn't believe in him or her, and now they must see what they passed up. Many times money make a person looks better, and that same person that you know who doesn't have money can be mistaken for some kind of bum or loser. But not only if you knew that they were worth millions, and it could make you very upset that you passed them up. For them this was their plan all along. Lastly it will make them look very attractive.

Jewel 345. Sometimes it's ten or twenty years down the road before we fully understand the psychological damage placed upon us as roots, and it's outcome. Family members are the worst ones that put us in this perpetual state of mind of hopes and dreams and rarely deliver the facts. We buy into the fool's gold of what their parents taught them and so on and so forth. When I was in prison a man told me that an incident changed him forever on the night before Christmas when he was being the average bad little boy as others were doing his time. He said he was in the closest looking for what he thought where presents in the closets. He said then like in a scary movie, he saw his mother dash in the darkness towards him in a frenzy and through black pepper in his eyes. When he told me, I laughed a little bit but then I stopped because I can tell he was still shaken up by this experience and he kept saying what made my mother throw black pepper in his eyes. I told him about the tales of Santa Clause and kids supposed to be in bed

When he came, but he said but I was her baby, and she threw black pepper in my eyes, I think she got scared took him to the doctor, but these are the deeply in rooted beliefs.

Jewel 346. Religion has it's place in history and in the world, And should be set aside to be used appropriately. But it should not be dealt with in a reference to a problem unless it can help the problem immediately. We live in a world that we throw religion on people and on a situation early and often as we can. The belief system is set up for those to believe and able to convert unbelievers if they are looking for some type of hope. When a person is hungry and needs funding, to tell him Jesus or Buddha bless you will only increase his hunger with frustration. Rather feed the man and then go on to tell the hungry what the feeding on the particular hope that you practice will do for him.

Jewel 347. It is not enough to say I'm going to get on a diet and then start running on a tread mill looking for results. It must be approached with a proper mind set and research that will make you successful. It took years of work to put weight on, it will surely take time to remove it. The fact of the matter is that every diet has its draw backs in trying to lose weight. A certain level of exercise is required alongside what you eat and even supplements, that will replace vitamins.

Jewel 348. Never become fixated by living in one place in the world, for boredom will surely find you in this house of misery, with you wishing to sale and get out. Rather put yourself in a position to live anywhere in the world you want and become and expert and fixated on what it is that people do that live anywhere in the world they want. Only then will you be happy with the house that you live in because, it will be exactly what you want. The world should be looked at as a smaller place than ever and especially when you see it from the heights of an airplane. Yet when we pick a community to live in, we must recognize that it is only temporary and that we may have to move the next day concerning our jobs, craft or other endeavors. The house we most time choose is something that we settle for at best, to live exactly where we want in what we want. It is impossible to be shown it on the market unless you are extremely lucky.

Jewel 349. Let us live with the mindset that even if we are winners, failure is so close around the corner that you can smell it, and never lose sight of failure. This can make us vulnerable and present weakness. Michael Jordan who is said to be one of the greatest basketball players of my father's generation. He believed no matter what the score was that it was 0-0 and the true score would be revealed as the buzzer sounded. Getting the first point on board meant a lot to him and he also recognized how easy it is to get comfortable with a lead and then blow the lead because in your mind you already won the game. The truth of the matter is as we see success around the corner, so is defeat. Even if it's only a few seconds away, never be too big in a rush to celebrate and even after the attainment of everything you fought for try all that is within you after the first 15 seconds of celebrations to return to humbleness and be grateful.

Jewel 350. The dangers of young girls to older men are these little risk takers will plot to expose what you think you are not, and then the moment they detect weakness, then they will run and tell the world of your mischief. They will giggle, flirt and smile coyishly at you only to seduce you to smile back and maybe say something that will be used in the court of law. This is the nature of girls to women understanding and developing what they may call power and homing in on feminine wilds. This is encourage by other young girls to see how productive their allurements are. It is only when the man fails that he realizes he's been played and how far do a young girl go to find out that she can no longer turn the man or does she go all the way and in her shame finding out feel dissuaded not to tell anyone.

Jewel 351. Money is only a symbol of success, true success is powerful and comes from a feeling of accomplishment. The measure money of money is just the biproduct of our development in disciplines to achieve our objectives. The true meaning of success is what type of influence do you have over the family, community, the world. When money is used to determining success then the world is screwed.

Jewel 352. There are some people that have the appearance of being touched with a stroke of genius, but if you use reason you will see a complete insane person. This is neither good or bad

if they are just insane, but you must be aware always if they are a criminal, manipulators, molesters, pedophiles, and cult leaders. They play to the audience and do the most outlandish and say the most unspeakable. It was reported that Malik Z York, born Dwight York, molested children in his community and also was said that he was an alien. It is most importantly not of accusations but the process of which men rise to power. It comes with seeing the genius in men and then the rationality of what it is that was first displayed becomes faded and frayed in the future.

Jewel 353. Goals should never vanish and disappear. They should only pile up on you to the point of suffocating you if you don't remove them one by one. So have the mind set to complete them or die with a thousand pounds on your chest. When goal are accomplished then they have the right to become a ghost. This means that 100 years from now, it has the ability to have it's presence felt. If you don't solidify the goals and objectives and just say away with it, then this is a major problem. You have become a winner at being a loser and will likely lose at more than just one goal or two. Yet if you decided that once you put an objective in front of you and it was vital that it get done, then that pressure will create a diamond in the raw. No stone un turned, no goals left undone.

Jewel 354. Never fantasize about the treasurcs of another in front of anyone. It makes you look tacky, classless, weak and pathetic. Do it alone on your personal time. Then use the visual to go after what you want. It should be embarrassing to look at another person possession and say out loud where people can hear, that you wish you had these things. Those that have no arms and legs have become very successful, so it gives me the understanding that you are a liar and really don't won't these things or you are facing mental challenges that prevent you of accomplishing the things that you see someone else has. It is better to say out loud these things are nice but I prefer to live more humble, and I could get those things if I desired them.

Jewel 355. A baby entry of the world is just as important as the old person going out. He or she must be seen after the honeymoon at birth as the clear object of what he or she shall

be. The out is the fulfillment of that hope. My daughter Chellsea called me just a few minutes ago and told me of her best friend Tayler Ray birthed a daughter into the world and at the moment she was in labor, the lights went out. This was said during the time by nurses that this hasn't happened in about 17 years. As the head came out, the lights came back on. This Trivial but profound symbol of greatness must be recognized early and often so that she may know, as well as all those that come in contact with her, that when she came into the world there was darkness, but when she came so came forth light. This is a remarkable way to see energy physically and spiritually brought forth.

Jewel 356. It has been said by some that if you are trying to accomplish a goal and it has a timeline of multiple years and it could have been done in a month to blow your brains out. I say the opposite to this scenario. Rather become obsessed of this goal to fulfill it in record time and see where that gets you. Its better to become a lunatic over being successful, than go crazy and not accomplish success and later blow your brains out any way. We are taking entirely too much time trying to accomplish our goals and objectives. What we said we would do five years ago should have only taking two months. People that start their own business are the worst in saying things like this or getting some type of license that they only have to study twenty pages for.

Jewel 357. Hurry and do what you are here to do on earth and off to the next life. It is a bad habit to think that we have all the time in the world, especially when we are young. Business owners should start recognizing if that is their path as children to go ahead and venture out, and get the education and experience along the way. It may be a spiritual path, or some other earth changing invention and then it's time to go. We probably live too long in terms of just being here and no longer having the drive to contribute on the world stage. You can be in only but so many relationships, experiences and other life moments, then the question will be evadible asked what is he or she doing here.

Jewel 358. Measure a man not by his character or personality only, see what others think of him also, in your final assessment.

It is true that we must go by a person character and personality, but it's nothing wrong with asking those close to the individual what are their thoughts. Then put together a timeline and story that you suspect would be reasonable to believe.

Jewel 359. Those that chase women instead of their dreams will always have to chase women, but for those who chase the dreams will have women chase them. Even when turning one down two will pop up to take her place. The reason why some become so successful is because of revenge. An extraordinary plot that has taken precision and discipline to get to that point. That was their dream to get to that point to have the last laugh. If that success is to achieve a relationship with a woman then the chase will always be on. If you chase the dream however, then the woman of your dreams will come find you. Others will hunt you down, stalk you, and find every psychotic reason to bump into you and be the one that you choose.

Jewel 360 Always write your goals and objectives down and carry them around in your pockets or wallet. Also have them in a place where you will see it every day. This will serve as a rendezvous point to the mind, till you can get them imprinted into your mind and then brought to the physical plane. In my pockets are my business cards of my business Measuring Stick 2 Success, and it has on the back one of my most sought after objectives. It's not to make $100,000 in a year, or have a woman who looks like Tara Banks, it is a quote by Steve Jobs—Be the yardstick of quality, because some people have never been in an environment where excellence is expected. I also have other quotes on my bathroom windows and put in drawers and different places that I will see every day. This gives me a fresh perspective every day of what it is that I must do so I don't grow comfortable going about my day.

Jewel 361.To be great you must find greatness in small portions and when you are great at something small. Now that you have something to compare to, you can use this for a larger vision of greatness. Once you see what it looks like you just duplicate the success. Small feat are just as important as the larger ones, because it will give you the blueprints to what it is that you must continue to do. Never despise the day of small beginning.

Jewel 362. Under mind what great thing you have set your-self up to accomplish. If I had to achieve a large task, like author 408 books, I would start off by saying all I have to do is write this amount or all I have to do that. Also anybody can do this and that, anybody can write a hundred books like flying a space ship or I'm I diagnosed with disabilities and handicaps. Make the task small and look at it as light work. If some has done it before then research them and find out what capabilities did they have so that you can possess them and go on to accomplish your agenda. So many people that have no arms or legs have went on to master great things, so the question will be what is out of your control and what can you control? What is wrong with you that you can't do what the next man does?

Jewel 363. Friendship has a price, a shelf life, and a paper trail. The price of friendship is being able to be used every now and then. If I can't use a friend to accomplish a service or act as I would for them, then they are useless. This is not a heavy price just the price of doing business as friends. The shelf life is when you think we can be friends and not utilize me a bit. An emotional deposit, or phone call, or some type of interaction. The paper trail is such as pictures of each other, financial favors, and tangible things passed and borrowed back and forth. Only this can fully establish proof of relationship, without this there is no friendship.

Jewel 364. Always have someone working for you even if it's hard to pay them for your services. First it's a good mental exercise to keep in habit with. When people do things for you that you can do for yourself, this is called delegation. It gives you the time to do the important things that you can only do. With this in mind lastly, it will create an opportunity to increase your finances so you can pay them more easily. This will become good practice the earlier you start this practice. It will free up so much time, that you will be able to accomplish the things that only you can do. That is why people that were striving to do great things like Steve Harvey, Eric Thomas, and many others went on to be success-ful because they was homeless living out of cars and abandon build-ings. This is because as they were perfecting their craft, they didn't have bills, a wife, or a stable relationship that had to be nurtured. It was all about this craft that they was trying to do. Since most don't have the luxury to not have bills or relationships, to balance it all will take help from those around you so you can put closer to 100% of your time into whatever it is that you are trying to do.

Jewel 365.25. Learn different languages, different religion, different cultures and history of different ethnic groups. Above all learn the language of finances for this will provide you the freedom to learn the previous spoken of in this Jewel. This will put you in position to never steal anything no matter how big or small. This is the plateau of elitism, being able to control what it is that you want to do with your life, in every aspect. To have all different perspectives of life will give the ability to know where you want to travel, what is it that you want to learn etc. etc. It will all come quicker when you understand the language of money so this new found freedom gives you the time to do all these things.

I Am Poetry

I am poetry, no one has ever been po'e as me
Low as me to go on 2 see what I would grow 2 be
When proses are read, its then they have read of me.
Red Roses and Blue Violets I hid in every tree
They couldn't see, Mind eyes in the forest hid
What society did is got rid of the kid in us
Adolescences crack the lid of strong drink, and cuss
In a rush we wanted bigger buss, eye shadow and blush
Thus, we lost intimacy and trust, and gained lust
Plus, the people of our times are disgusting to me
Roses that come after will be fresh as an evening breeze
Inside of these leaves, please seize the moment of poetry.

By Marvin Thomas.

lion head

a woman's greatest joy is to be destroyed and overpowered
hunted down like a wild animal and be explored and devoured
it's the hot sizzling pursuit that turns, her raging hormones on
dead locked eyez contact made intense sprayed pheromones
she can already feel this feverish heat, teeth mauling her insides
he smelled her from fifty feet, causing immense tingling vibes
she heard herself outer body with horrific
screams and sweet moans
his favorite parts are her inner hams,
upper shoulders and pelvis bone
for weeks he laid there, and watch and waited as he stayed there
she had no idea, just a feeling that this place he prayed there
no soon her scent carried in the air, he became wildly aware
imagine him racing through the woods, chasing to strip her bare
to ambush her with guards down her
musk precipitate to sweet linger
between his teeth slides pepto bismol pink
meat, spread by slipping in fingers
ohh how sweet is it to lick her, and puncture
her, and nibble leaving scars
this hunt has brought him to the closet he's
been to god in heaven thus far
as she lay out blood raw, ravished and
savagely stretched out naked
body language screams softy with a gasp
whatever you want just take it

By: Marvin Thomas

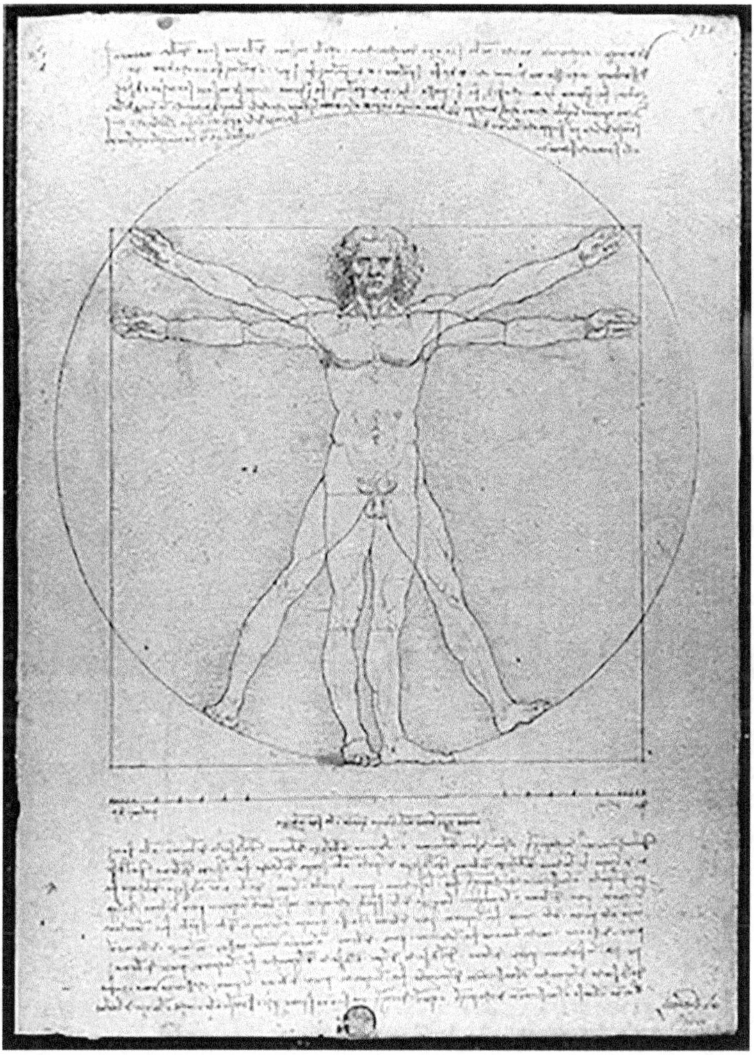

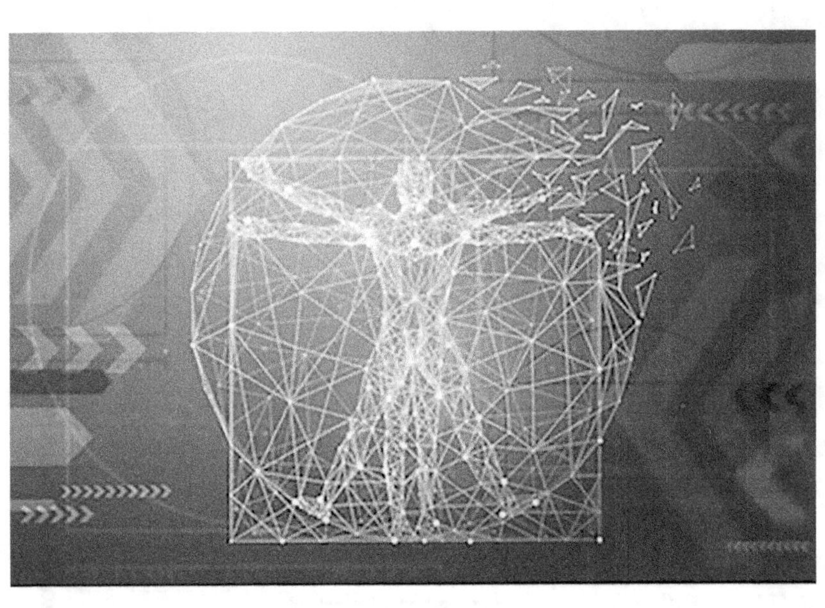

About the Author

Born in Williamston N.C. in 1976 started out as any other dusty country boy, running the fields with no shoes on with chickens and pigs as pets till it was time to eat them. He was raised with the help of a loving grandmother whom he called maowh. Which is country sounding for ma. To everyone else was known as Ethel Thomas, and courageous grandfather Henry Thomas, in the efforts to his mother Gloria Stokes provide financially and educationally. This was more than enough to succeed, but even with a structured family and sheltered in love, he decided to leave home at age 18 as the prodigal son did, with a few bags and started a journey that is still on today. With a lot of luck and prayers through marriages, jail, homelessness, prison and many near death experiences. Then as a light shine inside of all of this madness, it became clear as day that his purpose was to live free, to help thousands and leave his mark on the world. Now with multiple books published, two businesses established, a motivational speaker, college graduate with an MBA. These successes are mainly due to a beautiful woman he met in July of 2012 at the half-way house who believed in his journey. They soon got married and begin living a story united. She was one of the few that believed in his story. Marvin Thomas currently resides in Springfield Missouri.

everything is connected to everything

Presented by Marketing Solutions and Events

www.ingramcontent.com/pod-product-compliance
Lightning Source LLC
Chambersburg PA
CBHW051109050726

47592CB00002B/738